Save Our Strays

HOW WE CAN END PET OVERPOPULATION
AND STOP KILLING HEALTHY CATS & DOGS

Bob Christiansen

CLC Publishing

Published by
Canine Learning Center — Publishing Division
P.O. Box 10515, Napa, CA 94581
For orders please call: **1-888-434-3647**
Telephone (707) 226-5574
e-mail: rgc@saveourstrays.com

Publisher's Cataloging in Publication Data
Christiansen, Bob.
      Save Our Strays: How We Can End Pet Overpopulation
      and Stop Killing Healthy Cats & Dogs / Bob Christiansen -- 1st edition
      p. cm.
      Includes bibliographical references.
      ISBN 1-884421-49-0
      1. Animal welfare--United States. 2. Animal Shelters-- United States. 3.Title.
      HV4764.C47 1996   636.08'0973
                                 QB198-1762
Library of Congress Catalog Card No. 99-90101

Discounts of 50% off retail for bulk purchases of 12 or more books.

Visit our website at: saveourstrays.com

Table of Contents

Introduction 5

Origins of Animal Control and the Humane Movement 7

Current Surplus Pet Situation 11

The Right to Live, by Bernard E. Rollin, Ph.D. 14

The Dynamics of Surplus Cats 17

The Dynamics of Surplus Dogs 25

Factors that Save Animal Lives

    ☐ Effective leadership 31

    ☐ Effective community organization and program coordination 34

    ☐ Organizing a community coalition 46

    ☐ Proper data collection, scientific assessment of information, strategic planning and coordi-
       nated action based on findings 47

    ☐ Comprehensive, community spay/neuter programs 49

    ☐ Permanent identification programs 52

    ☐ Programs to deal with the uncontrolled reproduction of feral cats 54

    ☐ Responsibility and commitment by owners 58

    ☐ Balance of supply versus demand 62

    ☐ High-volume shelter adoption programs 63

    ☐ Curtail amateur and backyard dog breeding 64

    ☐ Programs to care for sick and injured animals 71

    ☐ Programs to detect owners who are uneducated or who are experiencing problems and to
       intervene with appropriate education 72

    ☐ Full support from the veterinarian community 73

       The Veterinarian's Role, Bernard E. Rollin, Ph.D. 75

    ☐ Educational programs to define the problem, prioritize resources and initiate solutions that
       change owner behaviors 78

    ☐ Animal legislation on which all organizations can agree 84

    ☐ Increase the supply of rental apartments and condominium housing where pets are allowed 90

    ☐ Better program accountability 90

    ☐ Shelters designed for group housing of dogs and cat colonies to decrease animal stress 94

    ☐ Productive economics 95

Conclusion 99

References 102

Appendix: Computing your regional statistics 103

Acknowledgments

I am deeply moved by the plight of orphaned animals. Many others share my concern for their welfare. It is troubling to know that most people need the companionship of a pet, but they are ignorant as to how to achieve it. Education is the vital link that will clarify the issues and provide the "Great Ah-ha" that will save animal lives.

I would like to pay tribute to the work of researchers who are referenced in the back of the book. In particular, I would like to acknowledge the work of Gary Patronek, Andrew Rowan, Phil Arkow, Joan Miller, Karen Johnson, Dr. W. Marvin Mackie and Merritt Clifton. These individuals have made significant contributions in the area of scientific research and evaluation of the surplus pet problem.

I would like to single out the work of Kim Bartlett and Merritt Clifton and their publication, *Animal People*. Their objective reports have cut through the confusion that surrounds the animal world and their publication has been a forum for factual discourse.

I would like to express my appreciation for the work of Richard Avanzino of the San Francisco SPCA and the Lewyt family who founded North Shore Animal League. They have demonstrated true leadership and provided a successful model for emulation.

This book was made possible by the professional contributions of Sharon Elwell, Ranny Green, Lana Denison, Kathy Burton, Karen Johnson, Bernard Rollin, Merritt Clifton, Jaye and Mac Horst, Reg Harris, and Joan Miller.

Finally, my gratitude widens to include all those thousands of people who give of their time and money, and who work tirelessly in the cause to save orphaned animals.

Front & back cover photos by: Jana De Peyer, POB 123, Kanab, Ut 84741
Inside photos by: Sumner W. Fowler, Marin Humane Society (unless otherwise marked)

Introduction

The pet population has doubled in the United States since the 1960s. The United States has twice as many dogs and cats per capita as the United Kingdom, four times as many as Germany, and five times as many dogs and eight times as many cats as Japan. Over 100 million Americans, living in 58.2 million households share a companion animal. We clearly love our pets. Or do we?

The relationships between Americans and their pets run the gamut of emotions. Some animals are embraced as cherished members of the family, featured in family photographs, sleep in the owner's bedroom and are deeply mourned after death. Others are kept isolated, "stored" in the backyard. All too often, when the human-animal relationship fails, a sequence of events is triggered which leads to the death of the animal.

Despite thirty years of intense effort at controlling pet population, euthanasia remains the leading cause of death among healthy and sound cats and dogs. Every day, our nation's animal shelters become the last resort for animals who just didn't make it in the family. Most people take on an animal casually, impulsively and uncommittedly. Many owners don't understand the animal and its needs. When the relationship sours, animals become "disposable items."

As the main repository for unwanted animals, shelters receive about 8% of the total household pet population. Due to a lack of space, 70% are euthanized.[1] In 1996, of the approximately 8 million dogs and cats received by shelters, 6 million were euthanized.

In the past, humane people have organized to correct public savageries to animals. When people became aware that dolphins were dying by the thousands in tuna nets, the outcry quickly changed the commercial tuna industry. It's heart warming that public outrage successfully reduced the slaughter of marine mammals. Unfortunately, the euthanasia of companion animals does not generate the same degree of outrage and indignation. Why are we less appalled that millions of healthy, sound companion animals are put to death each year?

The dynamics of the surplus animal problem are poorly understood by the general public. In a recent study by the Massachusetts SPCA, participants were asked to cite the problems associated with pet overpopulation. The most

When the "protector" serves as the institution passively cleaning up after the public, this grievously blurs moral distinctions and transforms non-profit animal welfare organizations from the last line of defense for animals to apologists who justify putting our friends to death.
— Ed Duvin

frequent response was "not enough effort to spay and neuter," followed by "animals running loose." Only 10% of respondents mentioned problems with over-filled shelters. Incredibly, only 42% of cat owners and 39% of dog owners are aware of pet-overpopulation problems.[24]

Although the number of animals euthanized has been significantly reduced since the 1970s, precious little scientific research has gone towards defining the problem or evaluating the effectiveness of existing intervention programs. Shelter statistics are randomly reported at national, state and local levels. Only a handful of communities have commissioned studies on pet and ownership dynamics that could define their regional problem more clearly. [37] In the absence of scientific analysis, even mainstay programs, such as low-cost spay/neuter, have come into question.

With the help of many caring individuals, several organizations have made significant progress towards lowering kill rates. Public and private funds have been efficiently used to lower the number of animal birthrates, increase adoptions and return animals home. Euthanasias have been held to a minimum. However, these practices have not been adopted consistently throughout the United States.

Shelter organizations typically view the problem as external. To what extent do poorly-run animal welfare programs contribute to animal deaths? When leading organizations have provided models for lowering kill-rates and their leadership isn't followed, to what extent are negligent organizations responsible for animal deaths?

We have reached a critical juncture in the struggle against pet overpopulation. From 1972 to 1992, with a combination of birthrate-reduction programs, education and heightened public awareness, we have drastically reduced the number of dogs and cats being euthanized. Had the percentage rate of euthanasia in 1998 remained consistent with 1973, we would be euthanizing 23.5 million dogs and cats, as opposed to 6 million currently.

From 1973 to 1991, we consistently made strides to decrease euthanasia. Since 1992 we have seen an alarming increase.

We have the means to end the needless killing of adoptable dogs and cats. A good home for every pet is possible if concerned animal lovers develop the infrastructure in their community to serve and protect pets. Progress can only come from a multitude of equally important programs. Each organization needs to clearly define its role and work together within those parameters.

The necessary resources, human and financial, exist. However, the problem of surplus pets does not have a quick-fix solution. Because the problem can never be entirely eliminated, only contained, preventative measures must be continually used to keep euthanasia rates at a minimum.

This report is a tool that communities can use to lower cat and dog death rates. It contains work from leading researchers on the subject of surplus pets. By adhering to these suggested recommendations, groups can set meaningful community goals, define objectives, and attain positive results.

Concerned animal lovers must unite and work productively to end the needless killing of animals in America.

*Animal advocates will be an
effective voice for animals
when actions reflect
a consistent and
uncompromised respect for
animal lives.*

Origins of Animal Control
and the Humane Movement

In the United States, after the Civil War, the public's compassion grew to include the plight of animals. Concern for animals was then, as now, far down on the ladder of social priorities. Humane reform developed when people could no longer tolerate the public savageries they witnessed to animals.

A few key individuals were prominent in arousing the public's consciousness. Their new moral ethic espoused a philosophy that promoted protection for the weak and oppressed. A philosophy emerged that included kindness, sympathy and mercy to less-fortunate beings who were being abused.

A New York ambassador, Henry Bergh, horrified at the sight of horses beaten in the streets, organized the American Society for the Prevention of Cruelty to Animals (ASPCA) in April 1866. He modeled the organization on a shelter he visited in England, the RSPCA. "Men will be just toward men when they are charitable toward animals," wrote Bergh. Soon other SPCAs were organized in Philadelphia and San Francisco by those who had heard of Bergh's work.

In March 1868, attorney George T. Angell, who had been outraged by the death of horses in an endurance contest, organized the Massachusetts SPCA. He also helped organize humane societies in Illinois, Wisconsin, Connecticut and elsewhere. By 1876, there were 27 humane groups from New Hampshire to California.

Animal problems started to mount when people moved off farms into urban areas, increasing the likelihood of unpleasant dog encounters. Local dog pounds, staffed by stereotypical dogcatchers, emerged and were paid bounties on every stray dog collected. New York City instituted a 50¢ bounty. In July and August 1867, New York officials impounded 5,825 dogs, which were thrown into large crates and lowered into the East River to drown.

Periodic "warfare" and lassoing "campaigns" by law-enforcement officials and cowboys against stray dogs in Tucson, Arizona left 106 dogs dead in one night, with a newspaper in 1876 observing, "This reduction in the dog population is a great relief, and the faithful officer who is accomplishing it deserves thanks and commendation."[5]

The community of nonprofit animal sheltering organizations potentially occupies the paramount position for being a powerful advocate and change agent for companion animals. But how persuasive can that community be when it speaks of qualities such as kindness, mercy and compassion to animals while still sponsoring the killing of those same animals? Can we believe that this contradiction is not lost on the public and does not seriously dilute the life-affirming message that we intend to send? If the message spoken by the animals' "best friends" is sufficiently diluted, is the solution to animal suffering merely prolonged? The public is sure to recognize at some level that not all of the animal killing performed at shelters serves the interests of animals as much as it does the interests of the public.

— Craig Brestrup

A number of societies extended the humane ethic to protect children from abuse, led again by the New York ASPCA. Because children were considered property in those days, there were no prohibitions against mistreating them. There were, however, laws against animal abuse. In the celebrated "Mary Ellen" case of 1874, a young girl was successfully defended in a child-abuse case because her attorney invoked the animal-protection law. It was argued that the little girl was, after all, an animal.

Rapidly, societies for the prevention of cruelty to children (SPCCS) were established. In 1871 the International Humane Society, which later became known as the American Humane Association (AHA) was organized to unify the growing movement to prevent cruelty to animals and children.

Many societies at the turn of the century provided care and shelter to stray and homeless dogs and cats. Some even employed a veterinarian. By the 1920s, some 36 shelters cared for America's orphaned pets. The numbers of nonprofit shelter facilities grew through donations and private funding.

In 1872 the mission of nonprofit humane work took a major turn. The Women's Humane Society of Philadelphia, frustrated because women were excluded from leadership positions at the Pennsylvania SPCA, became the first nonprofit organization to contract for animal control. Up until then animal control programs had always been government agencies with public employees, completely funded by tax dollars. In 1895 the American SPCA in New York followed suit by contracting animal control for New York City.

Four main factors induced nonprofits to change their mission. First, humane leaders were appalled by harsh conditions in government-run facilities. They believed government employees did not have the welfare of animals as their main priority. They thought they could do a better job. Second, many humane organizations were lured by the constant cash flow generated from government contracts, money they could use to support their work. Third, with animal control contracts came legal power, power that helped enact legislation and power that gave organizations legal-enforcement authority. Fourth, governments were highly motivated to subcontract animal control to reduce public complaints and ill will and reduce future costs (mainly salaries and benefits) associated with government-managed animal-control programs.

Unfortunately, animal-control contracts are not what they seem. Many humane organizations, frustrated by high euthanasia rates combined with a lack of adequate program subsidization, divested themselves of animal-control contracts. They discovered that income from government contracts (over the years) did not adequately cover expenses. They also found a growing public perception that they were the "bad guys" because of their role as government enforcement officers. This affected private fund raising efforts. Squeezed on the one hand by diminished funding and on the other by a constant flood of animals, they were incapable of helping, many renounced their government contracts.

In the 1950s, public animal shelters were working primarily to address the growing problem of rabies in wild and domestic animals. Many cities simply rounded up dogs and killed them to prevent free-roaming animals from spreading rabies. The Center for Disease Control recorded 7,344 domestic animal cases of rabies in 1953. In 1996, there were 574 cases reported in domestic species. Of these cases, 266 were cat and 111 were dog.

Rabies	1990	1991	1992	1993	1994	1995	1996
US Dogs	148	155	182	130	153	146	111
US Cats	176	189	290	291	267	288	266

To the general public and those in government, free-roaming animals were, and still are considered public-health risks. Laws and government agencies were instituted to "protect the people." Health concerns, primarily to prevent the spread of rabies and to keep the public safe from animal bites, took precedence over animal welfare.

As the surplus-animal population grew, it became a major concern for government officials. Mayors ranked animal-related issues as one of the chief annual complaints from citizens.

Government health agencies recognized a growing number of environmental and health issues associated with companion animals, particularly when these animals roamed the streets. (The incidence of dog bites is considerable, although many are not reported. Of the 2 million people bitten each year, approximately half are injured enough to seek medical attention. One fifth of the bites come from stray dogs. Dog bites are calculated to occur at a ratio of 1 bite for every 20 dogs.)[30]

The 1960s were a decade of rising crime rates and riots in the inner cities, which caused massive migration to the suburbs. Suburban households usually have larger yards and more space available for dogs. Combined with a need for personal protection, suburban life gave rise to an increasing demand for large dogs. The 10 most popular breeds prior to 1948 were mostly small breeds. Today the top breeds are Labrador Retriever, Rottweiler, German Shepherd and Golden Retriever, all large dogs.

The trend towards larger dogs created even more animal-control problems because larger breeds produce larger litters, are not as welcomed as their smaller counterparts in rental housing and are more prone to roam.

When greater concentrations of animals are brought into closer proximity with people, problems develop. In 1880, one in two Americans lived on a farm. By 1930, the ratio was one in four, and today it is less than one in fifty. People who migrated to the cities over the last hundred years did not leave the farm completely behind them. Today, more than half of American households keep pets.

In the late 1960s and early 1970s, angry citizens demanded that politicians do something about controlling nuisance animals and owners who refused to be responsible neighbors. The public expected governmental agencies to enact and enforce laws to resolve neighborhood conflicts and environmental degradation caused by free-roaming companion animals.

The educational function must be more aggressively undertaken by companion animal veterinarians. Animal welfare organizations only see a small portion of animal owners. The task of public education falls to veterinarians. In accepting this task, veterinarians could be a tremendous force for positive change.

Dog bites, free-roaming feral cats, zoonotic diseases such as rabies, lyme disease, etc., traffic, garbage scattering, nuisance barking, fecal deposits, and urine volume made animal control the number one complaint by citizens and fueled demand for better animal control, enforcement and legislation.

An increase in pet ownership in the late 1960s and early 1970s, combined with ignorance of animal birth-control methods, necessitated the killing of an extraordinarily large numbers of animals. The Humane Society of the United States conducted a nationwide survey in 1973 which revealed 13.5 million animals, approximately 22%, were killed in U. S. shelters.[43]

In the early 1970s the Humane Society of the United States, under the direction of Phyllis Wright, launched the Legislation, Education and Sterilization program (LES). The LES program marked a drastic change in approach to responsible pet ownership.[42] Prior to LES, education focused on teaching owners through gentle persuasion methods. After LES, there was more emphasis on local ordinances that urged *enforcement* and required pet owners to be responsible. This was a major shift in policy. Legislation and enforcement, education and sterilization have been promoted ever since.

Today, it is estimated there are some 4,000 animal-control and humane societies, with a combined budget of 2.7 billion dollars and a paid staff of almost 50,000 employees.

Historically, SPCAs made the tragic mistake of moving from compassionate oversight of animal-control agencies to operating the majority of kill shelters. The intentions were good, but the consequences in terms of resource allocation and sacrificing a coherent moral foundation have been devastating. The underlying dynamics that fuel overpopulation cannot be effectively addressed. The draining of nonprofit resources on traditional animal control functions, no matter how well-intentioned, ultimately serves to perpetuate the vicious cycle of killing good, adoptable animals.
— Ed Duvin

Current Surplus Pet Situation

According to David Hume, a Scottish philosopher and historian, the ultimate basis of morality was feeling: we act on our moral position because we are born with a psychological predisposition toward empathy or fellow feeling with other beings, because we are made uncomfortable by their suffering.

National Household Pet Ownership

	1970	1982	1984	1986	1987	1991	1996
Dogs							
% of Dog Households		40.5	39.4	38.7	38.3	36.5	31.6
# of Dogs (millions)	30.0	48.0	51.1	51.6	52.4	52.5	52.9
Dogs per household		1.44	1.51	1.51	1.51	1.52	1.69
Cats							
% Households		27.0	27.2	29.4	30.5	30.9	27.3
# Cats (millions)	32.0	43.0	48.5	56.2	54.6	57.0	59.1
Cats per household		1.98	2.07	2.16	2.04	1.95	2.19
Total Pets millions	62.0	92.0	99.6	107.8	107.0	109.5	112.0

The dog and cat population has grown from 62 million in 1970 to 112 million in 1996.[10] Despite a 90% growth rate in animals since 1973, the amount of killing fell from 13 million in 1973 to around 6 million animals in 1996 (5% of the owned population).[3] It was estimated that 21% of the dog and cat population was euthanized in the early 1970s. If educational and birth rate reduction programs had not been instituted and the rate of euthanasia had remained consistent with 1973, we would be euthanizing 23.5 million dogs and cats as opposed to 6 million.

Available national shelter statistics, based on random samplings, show little decrease in the percent of animals euthanized as a percent of animals impounded.[1] Nationally, shelters euthanize 61% of dogs and 80% of all cats that enter their facilities. Of the animals admitted, about 25% of dogs and 20% of cats are adopted. Approximately 14% of dogs and 2% of cats are returned to their owners.

Nevertheless, some well-managed agencies have reported substantial decreases in the percent of animals euthanized. Other agencies have decreased intake numbers and raised adoption and reclaim rates, resulting in fewer animals euthanized.

Researchers have noted that rates of killing are lower in the Northeast, higher in the Midwest, and highest in sun-belt areas of Florida, Texas and California. This may be do to weather factors and the ability of free-roaming cats to live through the winters.[3] In addition, researchers have found higher impound and euthanasia rates per capita in rural areas with farming cultures.

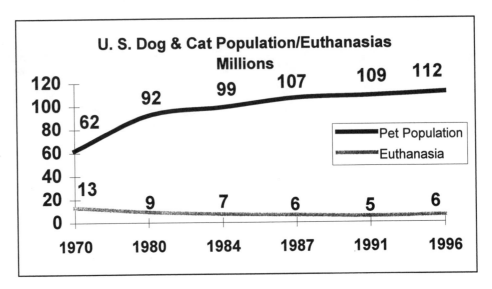

California Statistical Report 1970 - 1996

California represents 12.2% of the total U.S. dog and cat population 11.5% of total U.S. dogs and 12.8% of U.S. cats.[10] Canine impoundment at California animal-control shelters fell from a high of nearly 800,000 in 1974, to a low of 467,481 in 1992, a drop of 42%. Accordingly, euthanasias were also reduced, from 436,237 in 1970 to 276,789 in 1996, a drop of 36%.[12]

In 1970, the California animal population was 7.5 million; 1996, it reached 13.7 million animals: 6 million dogs and 7.5 million cats. Animal-control shelters admitted 502,491 dogs, or 8.2% of the owned population, and 392,099 cats or 5.2% of the owned population in 1996, for a total of 894,590 animals or 6.6% of the total population. Private shelters account for another 1.4%, bringing the total percentage to 8%.

In 1996, California Animal Control shelters euthanized 276,789, or 4.5% of the dog population, and 292,526, or 3.9% of the owned cat population. Euthanasias totaled 569,315 or 4.1% of owned dog and cat population within the state. If the rate of euthanasia was consistent with the early 1970s, California would be euthanizing 2.9 million pets, or 21% of the pet population.

Statistics show no significant progress in the reduction of shelter impoundments or euthanasias since 1992.

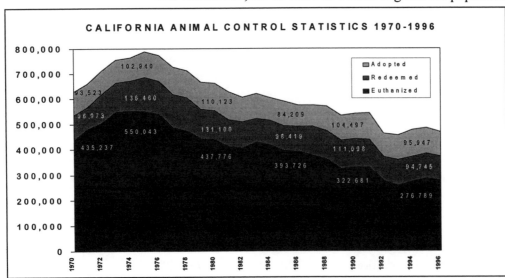

Further research reveals the inability of animal-control organizations to reduce euthanasia by increasing dog and cat adoptions or improving return-to-owner rates. Kill rates have been reduced over the last twenty years because fewer animals have entered shelters.

Most government animal-control organizations utilize their budgets in fulfillment of their mission of keeping the public safe from health risks by impounding free-roaming animals and responding to citizen complaints. Precious funding for proactive programs such as promotion of animals available for adoption and special programs to increase rates of lost animals returned to owners is seldom available.

Major Difference in County Euthanasia Rates

California has kept entry and exit statistics for more than three decades. Analysis of 1996 statistics shows a major disparity between suburban and rural counties. Most counties located in densely populated, metropolitan areas have relatively low impoundment and euthanasia rates compared to areas with less population density and stronger agricultural influence.

For instance, Los Angeles County euthanized 63,718 dogs or 3.9% of the total dog population in the county. Although Los Angeles County accounts for the highest number of dogs euthanized in the state, their kill rate is far lower than Fresno County, which euthanizes 22,597 dogs or 19% of their county dog population.

This is not a negative reflection on the animal-control shelters in agricultural counties. These facts reveal a social and cultural behavior in these communities that leads to the demise of close to 1 of 5 dogs and the need for proactive intervention programs in those regions. In the absence of these programs, animal control will be caught in a holding pattern and function to maintain the animal-carrying capacity by killing thousands of animals. These figures are consistent with rural agricultural communities throughout the state.

California County Dog Euthanasia Rate

Urban Counties	Rate	Agra Counties	Rate
San Francisco	0.86	Riverside	09.21
San Mateo	0.97	Butte	10.13
Marin	1.05	San Bernardino	14.11
Alameda	1.28	Tulare	14.26
Napa	1.81	Merced	14.35
Santa Clara	1.87	Yuba	14.98
Santa Barbara	1.94	Shasta	15.91
Orange	2.20	Calaveras	17.54
Sonoma	2.24	Del Norte	17.66
Contra Costa	2.44	Kern	17.94
San Diego	2.56	Fresno	19.04
Ventura	3.76	Kings	22.48
Los Angeles	3.97	Madera	23.92

The Right to Live

by Bernard E. Rollin Ph.D.

The traditional humane ethic emphasizes preventing animal abuse and encouraging kindness. Many people take that ethic even farther. By recognizing the sentient nature of our pet's; their ability to feel pleasure, pain, depression, boredom, joy, fear, anxiety, loneliness and stress, we give them a status equal in respect to humans. According to Hume, the ultimate basis of morality was feeling: we act on our moral position because we are born with a psychological predisposition toward empathy or fellow feeling with other beings, because we are made uncomfortable by their suffering.

The basic rights of animals involve a prima facie right to life and the right to live their lives in accordance with the physical, behavioral, and psychological interests that have been programmed into them in the course of their evolutionary development.

Animals, like humans, are morally important because what we do to them matters to them. The dog is essentially dependent upon humans for its physical existence, behavioral needs, and for fulfillment of its social nature. Cats also are interdependent, but in less overt ways.

The problem is not with dogs and cats, of course, it is with human beings. Companion animals are kept to bond with human beings, to give and receive love, loyalty, and companionship, and to enrich and deepen the texture of one's life. The nature of the relationship in its ideal form is not one of exploitation and profit, not one of possession, but of reciprocity.

Humans profit immensely from dogs and cats. There is overwhelming evidence indicating that lonely and sick people can enjoy immeasurable improvement in the quality of their life when they have a pet; something that needs them, something that will give and receive love. There is evidence that animals can speed healing, lower blood pressure and ease the pain of separation and the trauma of divorce.

Despite this pact, however, it is well-known that human beings often violate their part of the contract. The ways in which we fail to uphold our obligations to these animals are legion. We euthanize over 6 million healthy companion animals a year. Many of these animals are killed because owners are ignorant of the most basic aspects of animal behavior and cannot deal with minor behavior adjustments.

Pets are dependent on humans for their sustenance. As caretakers, humans need to be responsible guardians. Yet, the average person who buys or adopts a dog or cat is worse than ignorant -worse because they are invariably infused with outrageously false information. Information like: Cats suffocate babies. Dogs of the same sex will fight if put together. Purebreds are better than mixed breeds, Cats cannot be trained, Dogs need a big backyard. And, of course, the saying that prevents millions of adult dogs from being adopted, "You can't teach an old dog new tricks." The average person is either ignorant or misinformed about dog and cat behavior, training, biology, nutrition and in short, animal nature.

Owners are often ignorant of the animal's basic needs, such as food, exercise, personal attention, preventative medicine, the need for exercise and play. And, more sadly, owners lack commitment to resolve minor problems and lifestyle changes.

Veterinarians are an excellent source of information about the animal suffering that is engendered by human ignorance. All too often, a veterinarian is asked to kill a dog, sometimes a puppy, that is tearing up the house or barking while alone in the backyard.

The owner has tried beating, yelling, caging; nothing has worked. They are shocked to learn the problem was the dog was lonely.

In short, a major area of animal abuse in society is to be found in our treatment of companion animals. The abuse isn't an unfortunate by-product of some selfish goal. In fact, it is directly contrary to the intrinsic goal of pet ownership, that is, bonding with the animal, giving and receiving love, companionship and making the animal an integral part of one's life.

The documented pet abuse prevalent in society represents the worst sort of animal abuse, for it is totally wanton, senseless, useless and in direct contradiction to the basic reason for having a pet.

The majority of people are aware that dogs and cats die in animal shelters. We have become excessively familiar with the atrocities perpetrated on pet animals, so much so, that we take this condition for granted. We know intellectually this is intolerable. We know we are morally obligated to help, yet we are at the same time, strangely unmoved. The numbers are too large. The situation too emotionally charged, too depressing, so we turn away. The event becomes unconnected with our experience.

Most of the time moral blindness stems from a lack of familiarity. But other times, as in the case of pet animals, it stems from excessive familiarity. like people who grow up in cities that are not aware of noise until they visit the countryside and find it hard to sleep because its too quiet. Though we are dimly aware that millions of animals are killed, most of us take this as inevitable, albeit sad. We rationalize, hiding behind abstractions, like "euthanasia," "putting to sleep," "strays." If we are to effect our gestalt shift, if we are to see animals in the moral light which is there due we must recognize there right to life.

Here's a challenge. Take a few hours and visit an animal shelter. Choose a dog or cat that is scheduled for euthanasia. Choose a scruffy, homely, nondescript creature. Spend a half hour playing with it, pet it and talk to it. Let the animal respond to you. Watch the communication begin to flow, the rapport build, and a bond start. At the end of a half-hour return the animal to its cage, if you can. The concept of an animals right to life and the moral question of our responsibility for pet animals will never again be mere abstractions for you. And once the problem has assumed existential relevance for you, return to an examination of the theoretical and practical questions involved in what has come to be called "the pet problem."

We have here all the ingredients for moral awakening. All of us have or have known pets whom we have loved. All of us have the relevant information and experience - it only needs to be called to conscience. Few of us can fail to empathize with dogs and cats who are the actual cast of characters in this humanly created tragedy.

The problem of pet abuse will not be solved through sterilization alone. Although one can develop methods to spay and neuter multitudes of animals in simple and ingenious ways, this will not stop people from euthanizing animals for trivial reasons or failing to understand and provide for an animals' needs. These problems can be attacked only by changing the way people think, or more accurately, by getting them to think at all

To shift peoples gestalt one must strike at peoples reason and at their passions. Arguments alone do not move people; one must have an emotional pull toward actualizing the results of one's reasoning. People must be made aware of the philosophical principals, the moral theory underlying moral concern for animals. And further, they must be made aware of factual consequences of the pet problem: the animal suffering, the wasted lives and the dangerous example set for our children.

Bernard E. Rollin, Ph.D., professor of physiology and biophysics and director of Bioethical Planning at Colorado State University Veterinary School, is a world renown spokesperson on ethical animal issues. He is the author of Animal Rights and Human Morality.

The Dynamics of Surplus Cats

Ancient Egypt prized cats as symbols of fertility. Their ability to rapidly reproduce has been an evolutionary asset and essential to the survival of the species. Today, random and indiscriminate mating of unowned cats present one of the greatest humane challenges we currently face.
— Joan Miller

Just as cats are different from dogs, surplus cat dynamics are substantially different from surplus dog dynamics. Most areas in the nation are experiencing a critical cat overpopulation problem.

Cats have replaced dogs as America's most popular household pet. A 1996 survey commissioned by the American Veterinary Medical Association indicates there were 59.1 million owned cats living in 27 million U.S. households. The number of felines had risen since the last survey in 1991 but the number of households with cats decreased by 3.6 million. More multiple cat homes accounted for the increase in population.[10]

More often than not, cats find people instead of people making a deliberate effort to find a cat. Nearly 75% of cats are obtained in an unplanned manner. Only 13% come from animal shelters, 3% to 4% from breeders and 6% from pet stores. The majority are obtained as gifts or as strays who wander in and make themselves at home.[18]

The good news is people open their hearts and their doors to neighborhood free roomers. The bad news comes from people who don't care enough to spend money on veterinary care and, most importantly, sterilization surgery. Cats receive only about half the medical care that dogs receive.

If a cat is picked up by an animal-control officer, its chances of being claimed are slim. Only 2% are reclaimed by owners. An additional two out of ten are adopted, usually a higher number of kittens than adults.

Cat Lifestyles

"Between the truly feral cat existence and that of the pampered household pet, there is a continuum of lifestyles," according to Joan Miller, a renowned cat authority and director-at-large of the Cat Fanciers' Association.[29] To understand the nature of cats is to recognize the great diversity that exists within the species. Some cats are truly part of people's homes and lives, while others survive as ferals, avoiding humans and becoming a part of the ecosystem like raccoons, deer and other wild animals.

The basic rights of animals involve a prima facie *right to life and the right to live their lives in accordance with the physical, behavioral, and psychological interests that have been programmed into them in the course of their evolutionary development.*

– Bernard Rollin

Photo by Jana De Peyer

Some feral cats are commensal, that is, taking our food but continuing to live untamed and wild. Although the vast majority of cats has evolved to a fully domesticated status, others continue to hunt and roam freely, accepting food and limited protection from human beings when it suits them. Within a single species, there can be commensal and domesticated varieties. Juliet Crouton-Brock states, "Feral cats can exist wild as commensals, yet under domestication, cats can be so highly bred that they cannot survive without human protection."

The four main categories of the domestic cat are:

1. **Feral independent "wildlife" cats**
   Some feral cats are independent of human contact and live like wildlife. Their ancestry is feral and their behavior unchanged. Most have an evolved disease immunity and are self-sufficient hunters, completely avoiding humans, though some take food from humans. They go unnoticed by people, seen from a distance in the countryside. Their life is similar to any wild species, with seasonal fluctuations and availability of food source.

2. **Feral, interdependent free-roaming unowned cats**
   Feral and free-roaming cats can have an interdependent relationship with human beings. The ancestry of these cats may be feral or pet-reverted-to-wild. Their limited dependence on humans is motivated by a food source, and they will gravitate to a home-base, colony-type interaction. Some of these cats display an innate demand for more than food. They seek shelter, comfort and companionship.

3. **Domesticated, interdependent free-roaming loosely owned cats**
   These cats originate from the abandoned pet population, though some may be semi-tame feral cats. Their limited dependence on human beings is variable. They are tolerated in alleys, colleges, stadiums and other places for rodent control, but they are not "owned."

   Included in the two interdependent groups are managed, trap/test/vaccinate/alter/release (TVAR), maintained cat colonies; strays that live in many circumstances; doorstep colonies (several cats that are fed in backyards or near office buildings); porch cats that may be fed along with raccoons and other wild animals in outlying residential areas; and barn cats maintained on farms.

4. **Domesticated, owned household pets**
   Completely dependent, domesticated, owned cats, whether random-bred or pedigreed, are part of a household. These animals are referred to as pets because they are considered special and are cherished by owners. They have status because their needs are evaluated by their family when vacations are planned or other decisions are made. Their health is protected and they are fed well, groomed and receive loving attention every day. Some are allowed access to the outdoors because they will not tolerate an indoor-only lifestyle or because of their owner's attitude on roaming and perceived indoor boredom.

No one uniform entity can be defined as "the domestic cat." It is important to acknowledge the different segments of the cat population, understand their differing relationships with human beings and recognize the cats' ecological role.

Feral and Free-roaming Cat Colonies

Karen Johnson of the National Pet Alliance has documented the extent of the feral cat problem. Her studies concur with four other regional studies which found that stray, free-roaming and unaltered cats represent an additional 40% to 60% of the cat population exclusive of owned cats. These cats reproduce at will, having an average of two litters per year. If this overpopulation and reproduction problem is solved, it will drastically reduce the number of cats killed in shelters.

After a six-year study and daily observation of a feral cat colony, it was documented that stray female cats start having heat cycles when they are 4 to 6 months old, or as soon as days lengthen. January and February are the start of the breeding season. Litters are born from March through October (kitten season). Feral cats have an average of 2.1 litters per year of 4.25 kittens. Over half of all feral female cats are pregnant at any given time.

By the age of two months, 42% of the kittens will die. Of those that survive, many go on to perish in shelters. Those kittens that escape early death go on to bear, on average, four or five litters of kittens over their short life span. Only one in a hundred mothers live longer than three years.

Taking mortality into account, along with birth and death rates, the average stray female will have 5.3 litters in her lifetime, encompassing 22.3 kittens. At age two months there should be 12.9 survivors, roughly six females and seven males. These six females will go on to have thirteen surviving kittens each. Realistically, over three years, one unspayed female, with all her unspayed female offspring, can be responsible for over 800 kittens if there is no human intervention.

Cats are territorial. They don't allow other cats into their territory to steal their food. Altered cats will stand their ground and guard their food source, will not have kittens, and will die in a few years. Their population is self-regulating, similar to wildlife. Removing the cats from the habitat, without altering the food source, will not work. New, unaltered cats emerge and form colonies around food sources.

In 1994, a National Pet Alliance study of cats in California's Santa Clara Valley found that 37% of the impounded cats that were euthanized over an eleven-month period were either wild or unweaned offspring of feral and stray cats.[20] Once these wild kittens are over eight weeks old, they are highly resistant to socialization. An unsocialized cat is an unadoptable cat. Reducing the number of kittens born to feral cats would substantially reduce the number of cats euthanized.

Unowned cats are routinely euthanized at shelters. Even though the kittens can often be socialized for placement, it takes a minimum of two to three weeks of intensive work. Shelters simply don't have adequate time, personnel

Author Stephen Budiansky, in his book, Covenant of the Wild, *describes the concept of animal domestication as a coevolved relationship in which the animal species loses its defensive and self-sufficient behavior, in exchange for basic needs of food, protection and shelter offered by humans. Domestication involves a willingness on the part of the animal to adapt. The first animals to become domesticated were social, easy to tame, ready scavengers and accepting of dominance hierarchies.*

All animals should be altered before leaving animal shelters. In one study, 14% of the cats having litters prior to spay were obtained from shelters! Spay/Neuter contracts don't work.

or cage space to socialize kittens. Unweaned kittens are generally euthanized due to lack of foster homes, funds and space.

Stray cats produce more kittens than needed to sustain their population; they are also providing the balance of the kittens needed for households that own cats. Of course, the more human intervention in altering stray cats, the fewer kittens will be born. A large portion 82% to 86% of owned cats are altered. Most unowned and free-roaming cats are not.

The Touch Barrier

"There is a definite overlap in the various free-roaming categories, and some cats who have become accustomed to humans will revert to a more feral lifestyle if necessary for survival," according to Joan Miller. "Taming and placement of these cats is difficult, but possible, and their kittens can become household pets if socialized early enough. The primary demarcation that determines human relationship with these interdependent cats is a line called the "touch barrier." Cats that must be trapped to be handled will only be tamed

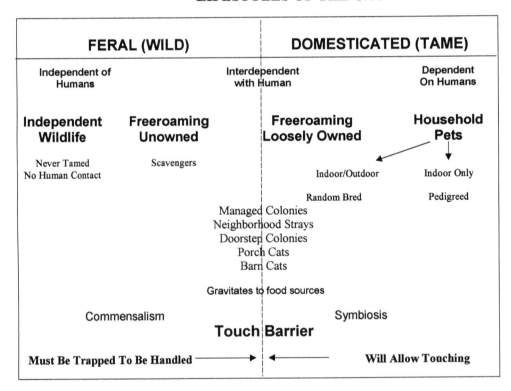

LIFESTYLES OF THE CAT

with a great deal of time and patience. When a cat or kitten will accept handling voluntarily, there is a chance that it can move from a free-roaming existence to that of a loosely owned or owned cat. Success in helping these cats will involve offering an attractive, safe environment and skill in taming."

Close to 70% of kittens obtained by households are coming from the feral population.
— Karen Johnson

Owned Cats

Owned cats produce only 22% of the kittens necessary to maintain the owned cat population at zero population growth. The large majority of household kittens comes from feral, free-roaming cat colonies.[20]

Only 3% to 4% of the owned cat population are pedigreed. There is no animal control problem with the pedigreed population of owned cats. Slightly over 1% of pedigreed cats surveyed were kept intact for breeding purposes. Through many years of selective breeding, most of the pedigreed cats' predatory instincts have diminished enough to enable them to be content inside, with human companionship and play substitutes. Owners of pedigreed cats rarely allow their pets outside of home confinement, nor will these cats care to go out. If these cats are bred, they produce wanted litters.

A San Diego, California study revealed 6.4% of owned cats disappear for a day or more. Nearly three-quarters return home on their own. Of those who remain missing, 14.8% are never found despite the fact that every owner had visited the shelter. Between 1% to 3% of owned cats permanently stray. It was calculated that permanently missing cats accounted for .9% of the entire owned cat population. Around 14.5% of the owned cat population dies every year.

The ratio of sexes in owned cats is 50/50 initially, but by the time the cats are ten years old, the ratio is 70% female, 30% male. Unowned cats at ten years are 35% females, and 65% males.[20]

Sterilization

Four separate studies: Massachusetts, Santa Clara, CA, San Diego, CA and Las Vegas, NV found that between 86% and 91% of owned female cats were spayed. However, somewhere between 16% and 20% of owned cats have one or two litters prior to being altered. More owners of sexually intact cats cited cost as the reason for failure to sterilize cats.

The Massachusetts SPCA conducted a phone survey of people who advertised free kittens in the Sunday paper. The survey revealed that most of the owners (72%) considered having the female spayed but procrastinated, thinking the female was too young to give birth. Most of the litters born to owned cats result from accidental breeding. People were simply not aware that cats can become sexually mature quite young. An education program targeted at this problem is in order. Education has already been shown to be effective in other areas of pet ownership. Legislation will not prevent well-meaning, but uninformed, pet owners from having accidental litters.

The Egyptians revered their cats and admired their ability to see in darkness. They believed cats would lead them through the ultimate darkness, death. A cat's luminous eyes would guide the way.

Many studies have shown early surgical altering of cats is safe, a fact not known by all veterinarians. Veterinarians usually recommend spay/neuter at six to eight months, months after female cats can mate. This overlap period is the time when many accidental breedings occur. Veterinarians need to be at the forefront of educating their clients.

All animals should be altered before leaving animal shelters. In one study, 14% of the cats having litters prior to spay were obtained from shelters![20] Spay/neuter contracts don't work. Policies should immediately be changed to adopt and release no animal who has not been spayed or neutered. In effect, shelters are now responsible for one in seven litters which contribute to the surplus pet problem. This is unacceptable.

Relinquishment

Cats are free spirits, independent, and somewhat mysterious. Those of us who love cats truly appreciate the essence of the feline nature. We love the beautiful feline physical attributes, the luminous cat's eyes, the grace, agility and alert reactions. We admire cats' aloof, free-spirited yet affectionate nature. Cats' physical and behavioral traits have been admired by civilizations throughout history. These characteristics, although responsible for a cat's cunning ability to survive, can be the very same qualities that contribute to people's indifferent attitudes and cause various problems in the human-cat relationships.

Cats are cautious creatures. There is not always an immediate welcome. Cats are protective of their territory, generally prefer familiar routine, and are sometimes aloof from or fearful of newcomers. With time and patience, however, cats adapt to new environments, new people and other animals. Felines have an innate desire for companionship, some more than others. With considerate handling, a cat's affection will be drawn out.

While many people admire a cat's free and independent spirit; others dislike these qualities and the difficulty of controlling these animals. Cats have always elicited powerful feelings and emotions in human beings. It is not easy for some to understand or appreciate a judgmental, decision-making animal that is not submissive to human will.

When owners have an unfulfilled expectations about the cat's role in the household, relinquishment is likely. Some new cat owners may have unrealistic expectations about the characteristics of cats as pets. This, understandably, should be addressed before the cat is adopted for educational intervention to be successful.

The top ten reasons why cats are relinquished to shelters[44]

1. Moving
2. Landlord does not allow pets
3. Too many animals in household
4. Cost of pet maintenance
5. Owner has personal problems
6. Inadequate facilities
7. No homes available for litters
8. Allergies in family
9. House soiling problem
10. Incompatibility with other pets

Risk of Relinquishment Factors for Cats

From a study by Gary J Patronek, VMD, Ph.D.; Lawrence T. Glickman, VMD, Ph.D.; Alan M Beck, ScD; George P McCabe. Ph.D.; Carol Ecker, DVM.[39]

Increased Risks of Relinquishment	Decreased Risk of Relinquishment
Greatest for cats less than 6 months old	Declawed
Sexually intact	Found as strays
Mixed breed	Unexpectedly acquired
Acquired at no cost	Pedigreed
Never visited a veterinarian	Owner who read a book
Inappropriate scratching	Spent time inside home
Inappropriate elimination	Cared for by entire family
Owner's inappropriate expectation	Greater owner investment
In households with children	Spayed/neutered
In rental housing	Housebroken (uses the litter box)

Behavior problems

The number one behavior problem that leads to relinquishment of a cat is house soiling. A fresh daily litter litter box will help curtail this problem. Cat scratching can be destructive and also lead to relinquishment. Scratching is natural and instinctual, involving not only visual marking but an attention-getting, happiness display. Ideally, this behavior should not be stopped, but channeled to acceptable surfaces, such as cardboard and rope posts. Routine trimming of the nails and claw guards are alternative solutions.

The Cat Fanciers' Association (CFA) disapproves of declawing cats and severing the digital tendons on grounds that it is without benefit to the cat. The American Veterinary Medical Association's policy is: "The declawing of the domestic cat is justifiable when the cat cannot be trained to refrain from using its claws destructively."

Confinement

Cats are great hunters. They are genetically programmed for specific predatory work and the feline personality has remained strongly connected to this function. Knowledgeable cat owners offer stimulating indoor environments that keep their cats safe from harm and satisfy their fundamental hunting instincts. Unfortunately, many cat owners find it difficult to confine cats that exhibit strong desires for the outdoors. On the one hand they desire to have their cats safely indoors; on the other they acknowledge their cat's desire for the outdoors and let it roam.

The ideal is for cats to be indoors only, but that is not always easy. Domesticated pets with a hunting instinct will feel less stress inside when owners provide a stimulating environment.

Tips to Keep a Cat Indoors

1. Spay/neuter your cat.
2. Build a shelf or high perch so the cat can see outdoors.
3. Provide a scratching post.
4. Trim your cat's claws regularly.
5. Clean your cat's liter box daily.
6. Provide safe toys and boxes.
7. Spend quality time with your cat.
8. Consider having two cats.
9. ID your cat.

If you insist on letting your cat outdoors, make sure your cat stays indoors at least 2 months before you release it. Reward your cat when it returns.

Two California studies, in San Diego and Santa Clara, revealed where cats were allowed to reside.

	Indoors Only	Outdoors Only	Indoors/Outdoors
Santa Clara	33.3%	14.2%	52.5%
San Diego	37.2%	17.4%	45.4%

The Feeding of Strays

Approximately one of ten households feeds stray cats. These strays, when added to the known owned cat population, represent between 36% and 42% of all known cats. Only 7% to 9% of all households that were feeding strays had altered them. The number of cats fed but not owned ranges from 2.6 to 3.7 cats per household. Of fed strays, 18.5% were known to have kittens.

The Ultimate Goal

An active community program should identify the source of the threats to the well-being of cats and implement plans that safeguard their survival.

Photo by Jana De Peyer

The Dynamics of Surplus Dogs

Nationally, the supply of puppies born each year is close to being balanced with the demand, although regional imbalances persist. Unfortunately, millions of dogs still die in shelters each year. Efforts to curb this crisis needs to refocus on the reasons why dogs are being euthanized.

Dogs have been domesticated and served humans for more than 12,000 years. Domestication implies a human attachment in which the canine loses its wild, defensive and predatory behaviors in exchange for fulfillment of its physical, behavioral and social needs. Throughout the ages, dogs have helped man in his daily life. Today, humans agree to provide for a dog's needs in exchange for friendship and companionship. Generations of selective breeding have made the domestic dog incapable of survival outside of human society and dependent on man.

The dog's natural pack structure has been integrated into human society, with humans playing the role of pack leader. Dogs have served man as guardians, sentinels, herders and hunting guides. Dogs have warmed our cold nights, guided our blind, comforted our lonely and relaxed our stressed. They have served in numerous utilitarian ways and touched our hearts with their sentient nature and steadfast loyalty.

Humans profit immensely from the association. Dogs, however, haven't benefited as well. The ways in which man has betrayed these creatures are numerous. When the bond of mutual attachment fails, it is very threatening to a dog. Their genetic programming does not allow for abandonment. For dogs, to be expelled from the pack is a life-threatening situation.

The main factors that lead to the premature death of dogs

1. Failure to properly train and integrate the dog into the home
2. Lack of identification to reunite lost dogs with their owners
3. Failure to spay or neuter
4. A prejudice against mature dogs (over 1 year of age)

*Gentleman of the jury:
The one absolute unselfish friend that man can have in this selfish world, the one that never deserts him, the one that never proves ungrateful or treacherous, is his dog. A man's dog stands by him in prosperity and in poverty, in health and in sickness. He will sleep on the cold ground, where the wintry winds blow and the snow drives fiercely, if only he may be near his master's side. He will kiss the hand that has no food to offer, he will lick the wounds and sores that come in encounters with the roughness of the world. He guards the sleep of his pauper master as if he were a prince. When all other friends desert, he remains. When riches take wings and reputations fall to pieces, he is as constant in his love as the sun in its journey through the heavens.*

— Tribute to the Dog

Dog Training Basics

1. Have a reasonable expectation that it will take time for the dog to adjust to its new home.
2. Start training early, as soon as you obtain the dog.
3. Prevent negative behaviors and reinforce positive behaviors.
4. Try to understand the thinking behind the dog's actions.
5. Teach the five basic exercises (heel, sit, stay, down and the recall).
6. Always train using a leash.
7. Keep your voice firm with commands, higher with praise and lower with correction.
8. Have tolerance for problems and confidence they will be worked out.
9. Be consistent.
10. Praise and correct immediately.

Training should be fun. Use tiny food treats to motivate and reward.

Behavior

Most owners (84%) acquire a dog as a puppy.[33] Many of these new owners are filled with misguided folklore and myths regarding the training and handling of a dog. Only a small percentage of people seek professional training. Most people do it themselves — and they fail.

Successful adopters have *reasonable expectations* for the roles their dogs will play in their lives, and therefore develop strong attachments. Well-prepared owners are able to devote time to nurture and train their pets. They understand the money, time and care-taking commitment that pet ownership demands. They anticipate undesirable behaviors and are willing to learn techniques that modify and eliminate problems.[21]

The key for most dog relationships is to integrate the dog into the home and make it part of the family. Certain behaviors, which are natural to a dog (barking, chewing, digging, excreting, mouthing) must be modified for the relationship to work. For instance, since dogs need to excrete, they will go inside the house until they are instructed otherwise. Dogs need to chew, but chewing on the new pair of Italian loafers is unacceptable. Learning what is acceptable is required for dogs, who have an innate ability to want to please their masters.

Owners can control their dogs when their dogs are puppies. As the dogs grow and reach the adolescent stage, they becomes more willful. People who fail to properly train their dogs find that minor problems become more pronounced as the dog matures.

The vast majority of these behaviors are normal to a canine but unacceptable in human households. Often, people lack the understanding to direct the dog to more acceptable behaviors. As a result, the relationship grows bothersome, dog owners spend less time with the dog, which only exacerbates the problem. The relationship fails, and the dog is soon relinquished.

Neglect is the root of many behavioral problems. Dogs, after all, are social animals. It's unnatural for them to be alone. Many adolescent dogs react negatively to isolation by barking, chewing, digging and trying to escape. In the absence of proper training, dogs can exhibit anxiety through destructive behaviors like chewing the couch. Dogs who are left alone and not properly socialized and trained become fearful. Usually, this leads to more isolation and eventual relinquishment.

Approximately 8% of the total dog population (4.2 million dogs) enter animal shelters in America.[37] Of those animals, 60% (2.5 million or 5% of the owned population) will be killed. The overwhelming majority of the dogs killed are not puppies (as would be the case if there were true dog overpopulation) but young adults who were once owned.

Most shelters have a shortage of puppies. Some, usually in agricultural areas, still see an abundance of litters. In some cases, puppies are transferred to areas in order to fill high demands.

There is a significantly higher rate of euthanasia for mixed breeds compared to pedigreed dogs; pedigrees are reclaimed at much higher rates. Pedigreed dogs from the Sporting group were over-represented as strays, accounting for 40% of purebred stray dogs, even though they only account for 25% of the purebred dog population.[36]

The turnover in dog ownership in the United States is about 7.8 million animals or 14.8% annually. Animals that don't go to shelters are given away or sold to friends, relatives and neighbors. According to Gary Patronek, an expert in pet-population dynamics with Tufts University, there are approximately three times as many owners relinquishing their dogs as breeding.

To put the relinquishment problem into perspective, only one out of three dogs will live its entire life with its original owner. When people decide they can no longer keep the dog, they try various means to find it a new home. They place ads in the local newspaper; they beseech friends, neighbors and relatives. When all else fails, they either take the dog to the shelter or let the dog loose with no identification.

Risk of Relinquishment for Dogs[52]

Increased	**Decreased**
Sexually intact	Helpful advice (94% lower risk)
Lack of veterinary care	Participation in obedience classes
Dogs obtained at little or no cost	Dogs that received veterinary care
Dogs that spent most of the day in the yard	Dogs considered family members
Less family interaction	Owners older and more mature
Owners find dog more work than expected	Purebred
Younger, poorer and less educated owners	Decreases as the animal matures
Owners who are moving or getting divorced	Spent a portion of the day inside
Dogs that soiled or damaged the house	Stronger attachments
Owners who are losing a job	Acquired from a pet store
Dogs that are hyperactive or noisy	Housebroken and quieter
Living in rental housing	Owners more affluent and stable
Households with children	More financial investment
	Neutered or spayed dogs

Once people take an animal to a shelter, they are more likely to repeat relinquishment than someone who has never done so.[44]

Identification

Our current public dog identification system is a major failure and results in millions of dogs being killed every year. The majority of dogs that enter shelters are classified as strays (dogs with no identification). In California, close to 75% of all dogs that enter animal control shelters are strays.[12] They were either picked up on the streets by animal control officers or were brought in by good Samaritans who found the dog running loose. An effective identification system would cut the canine kill rate in half.

Shelters have a poor record of recycling dogs back into the community. Some 75% of people who relinquish their dog to a shelter do so with the expectation the dog will be adopted. The fact is, only one of four will be adopted (usually younger and smaller dogs). Only 13% of dogs are obtained at shelters. There are many reasons for poor adoption rates, some having to do with the institutions, others with public perception.

Homer's Odyssey *relates one of the most famous of dog stories, that of the faithful Argus, a favorite hound of Odysseus. Old, neglected, lying on the dunghill of the gate, Argus was the only one to recognize Odysseus on his return home after a nineteen-year absence.*

Shelter management has historically resisted traditional business practices. As a result, marketing, advertising, public relations and customer service programs are underdeveloped. Many facilities look and feel like prisons. They are poorly lit, loud and smelly. People are left on their own to view and evaluate the animals, which can lead to misunderstandings. Many people, for example, see a barking dog as undesirable, when it may just be barking for attention.

The success of mobile adoption centers, like PetsMart and Petco, which have accounted for more than 200,000 adoptions, proves that people will adopt orphaned dogs if the animals are presented in a pleasant surrounding.

Most people avoid shelters simply because of the environment. They become depressed at the thought of viewing dogs on "death row." There is also a public perception that dogs in shelters are "bad dogs" and that shelters are doggy prisons. These perceptions must be changed to increase adoptions.

Adult Dog Prejudice

The public has a strong desire for puppies, but the majority of dogs entering shelters are 7 to 18 months of age and older. Until the image of adult dogs changes, dogs over 1 year will continue to be killed. [38]

A Humane Society of the United States survey revealed 53% of respondents would still not adopt an adult dog, even after they were told of the benefits. They objected because of the old myth, "You can't teach an old dog new tricks" (40%), "less fun" (12%), "trouble adjusting" (10%), "not good with kids" (6%). Certainly public information campaigns that address the misconception about retraining older dogs are needed. [18]

Spay/Neuter

Spay/neuter surgeries have dramatically reduced the numbers of litters dumped at shelters. Spay/neuter education and low-cost programs have resulted in close to 63% of all dogs being altered, although some had a litter prior to being altered. Of the dogs that are unaltered, about 5% have litters.

Breeders

The breeding of pedigree dogs, contrary to popular opinion, is only a minor factor in the surplus dog problem. Purebreds, which represent 55% of all dogs in America, are under represented in shelters. Only about 20% of dogs in shelters are purebreds and a much smaller percentage are killed, mainly due to public demand and purebred rescue efforts.

There are still deeply held beliefs that breeders are the source of the problem and breeding of any kind cannot be condoned. Major national groups have been beating that drum for a long time and are finding it difficult to change their position, despite scientific evidence that states otherwise.

We will decrease the rate of dogs killed in shelters when our educational programs reach owners *before* they obtain a dog and during the critical first year of ownership. Looked upon as authority figures by the general public, veterinarians play a crucial educational role and are key to the success of the human-pet relationship. Expectations must be aligned, commitment established and responsibilities learned. The adolescent and adult dogs in shelters are victims of people who did not understand the realities or think through the responsibilities and duties of pet ownership.

Programs that Save Animal Lives

1. Effective leadership
2. Effective community organization and program coordination
3. Proper data collection, scientific assessment of information, strategic planning and coordinated action based on findings
4. Comprehensive, community spay/neuter programs
5. Permanent identification programs
6. Programs to deal with the uncontrolled reproduction of feral cats

7. Pet Retention
8. Balance of supply versus demand
9. High-volume shelter adoption programs
10. Curtail amateur and backyard breeding
11. Programs that care for sick and injured animals
12. Programs to detect uneducated owners or those experiencing problems and intervene with appropriate education
13. Full support from the veterinary community
14. Educational programs that define the problem, prioritize resources and initiate solutions that change behaviors
15. Animal legislation on which all organizations can agree
16. Increase supply of rental apartments and condominium housing where pets are allowed
17. Better program accountability
18. Shelters designed for group housing of dogs and cat colonies to decrease stress.
19. Productive economics

SAVE OUR STRAYS

Spay/Neuter

Low-Cost Spay/Neuter Clinics   Mobile (cat only) Spay/Neuter   Vouchers   Government Subsidy
Spay-a-thons & Spay Days   Feral Cat Spay/Neuter   Program for People Who Feed Stray Cats

Permanent Identification

PET RETENTION

Align Expectation   Crisis Intervention

TRAINING

Regional Goals

Early Age Spay/Neuter

Increase Demand for Mature Shelter Dogs & Cats

Data Collection & Analysis

ORGANIZATIONAL PRODUCTIVITY

Aggressive Shelter Adoptions

Proper Funding For Animal Programs

Local Breed Club Certification

Veterinarian Involvement

Trap Vaccinate Alter Release Maintain

FERAL CATS

Factor One
Effective leadership

Situation

A Question of Leadership (National)

The first lesson to learn in stopping needless companion-animal death is that no single person or group can solve the problem alone. It's too big. We need each other to be successful. Unfortunately, animal-related groups have not been successful at organizing, forming coalitions, reaching consensus and working together to end this tragic problem. Why?

Leadership is defined as the act of being the first or the principal performer of a group. One of the major reasons why millions of animals die is a failure of national organizations to be leaders — to properly define the problem, form a solution and communicate a program to grassroots America that unites communities in the common cause of ending needless animal killing.

Animal groups that should be getting together and working to solve the problem are instead being singled out and accused of wrongdoing without concrete evidence. Gut feeling and emotion reign. Veterinarians are accused of being greedy. Pet stores are accused of selling dogs that come from puppy mills. Dog trainers are charged with ineptness. AKC purebred dog breeders and CFA pedigreed cat breeders are singled out as culprits for bringing animals into an already crowded world. Animal control programs are viewed with contempt and accused of nonchalant performance. Humane societies and SPCAs are accused of being self-righteous bleeding hearts that would rather kill an animal than give it to a person who doesn't meet their high standards.[49]

Unfortunately, major organizations have embarked on policies that have polarized people. Instead of using resources to conduct scientific research to formulate policy based on facts, they have embarked on campaigns based on anecdotal information that radicalized issues and alienated mainstream animal groups who have an avid interest in solving the surplus animal problem. The nature of debate is often emotional, irrational, and prone to distortions. Overblown euthanasia statistics are used to support political agendas.

In the early 1970, the Humane Society of the United States (HSUS) under the direction of Phyllis Wright launched a program called LES. The acronym stands for Legislation, Education and Sterilization. While HSUS should be commended for its stance on sterilization and education, legislation as a means to combat overpopulation has not proven to be effective and, often is counterproductive to united resolve.

The LES program marked a drastic change in approach to responsible pet ownership. Prior to LES, humane education primarily focused on gentle persuasion methods. After LES, there was more emphasis on local ordinances that impelled *enforcement* requiring pet owners to be responsible. This major shift in policy persists to this day.

Because legislation and enforcement are major tactics of animal-rights activists, other organizations have had to step up their legislative activities to represent and defend their positions. The result is a major stalemate. Large sums of money that could be benefiting animals are being wasted.

[An] unintended consequence [of nonprofit animal-welfare agencies practicing animal control] is that open-door policies inadvertently reinforce the idea of animals' disposability. When a full shelter continues to take in animals, one must question the priorities of this helping profession toward existing and potential "clients." Helpers of humans have uniformly favored the welfare of existing clients, while animal shelters have taken the more expansive position of serving all comers, even when that means killing some to make space. I submit that this looks like what it is: a betrayal of the animals already taken into care. Nonprofit animal welfare contradictions go to the heart of the enterprise and help to defeat its larger purposes and subvert its deepest values. We cannot condemn killing with one voice while doing it and defending it with another without sinking into apparent incoherence.

– Craig Bestrup

Life itself remains the grand reality, and its value should not be obscured to the point that respect boils down to just attending to life's gentle passage into death. If those who include non-human animal life within this expanded purview wish to be persuasive with that conviction, they have great reason to re-evaluate their bearings, methods, and ultimate aspirations.
— Craig Brestrup

Puppy mills appall every humane-minded person. Their practices are despicable. Why haven't these practices been stopped despite almost thirty years of legislative and enforcement efforts? Could it be these tactics don't work?

Major organization undoubtedly believes that legislation and enforcement will make everyone behave. They have an obvious agenda to usher nonprofits into more animal control and enforcement activities.

Recently, HSUS and the American Humane Association (AHA) took a controversial stance against feral cats by siding with the American Bird Conservancy, which accused feral cats of diminishing the population of some songbirds. There are significant studies that prove otherwise. Failure to act prudently will give animal control more reason to aggressively use trap and kill methods, including managed colonies that have been trapped, spayed/neutered and released by humane cat lovers.

No major for-profit business would initiate a new product or major policy shift without first doing scientific research. There is an information black-hole existing today within the animal-shelter world which causes agencies to operate in the dark and make decisions without all the facts — decisions that best suit their agenda. This inhibits productive development.

A Question of Leadership (Local)

Boards of directors are the governing bodies of humane organizations. Directors have the power to save millions of animal lives in America or squander precious assets. They act to ensure the organization uses its resources in the fullfillment of its' mission to help homeless animals. Their responsibilities center on two main areas of activity: governing the organization including program and financial oversight and supporting the organization through fundraising, public relations and other work. A governance board gives direction to staff through program planning and formulating policy, assists staff with the implementation of those plans and then evaluates results.

Unfortunately, not all boards function to the full extent of their capability. This problem is inherent in the nonprofit organizational structure. The vast majority of board members are competent and well-meaning individuals who generously volunteer their time and services. They come to the board from various backgrounds "to help the animals." Generally, their commitment is limited to 10 hours per month.

Although power is vested with the board, most directors know very little about the true role of a nonprofit animal-welfare organization and animal-shelter management. They are often uncertain about their role and how to be effective. This causes differences of opinion to develop. When they take time to investigate operations they are accused of "micro-managing," meddling and stepping on the toes of the staff.

Board members rely on information from the executive director, which allows the executive director to frame the discussion in a manner which best suits his/her point of view. Board members can often be overwhelmed by superior knowledge of shelter affairs and defer their judgments to "higher authorities."

The executive director's role in managing the organization and assisting the board is perhaps the most paradoxical of all relationships in the nonprofit sector. The executive director's responsibilities are to deliver the programs and policies that the board authorizes and operate the business of the agency. On one hand, the board as the "boss," plans and directs the organization's vision. On the other hand, the executive director informs, advises and provides leadership to the board and directs the staff. An executive director, no matter how talented, can never accomplish as much in the community as the full power of the entire board. Nor can a strong, committed board operate programs, be as knowledgeable on industry issues or maintain proper supervision, as well as the executive director.

In most mature organizations, the role of governance has diminished and the board's activities focus almost entirely on fund raising and support. These boards still have the same legal and formal responsibilities as other boards, but perhaps because the organization has been stable and unchanging for some time, or perhaps because the organization is formed around the vision of a strong-minded president or, executive director, the role of a board member is almost entirely that of supporter and fund-raiser.

Problems can develop on several fronts. When program performance flounders, most board members are either unaware of the situation or lack sufficient knowledge for corrective recourse. Normally, when adequate funds are received and entry and exit statistics are similar to the previous year, it's business as usual.

Strong boards that increase organizational capacity are critically important in the long-term fight for animal welfare in our communities. The challenge for governance boards is to avoid becoming too removed from the issues and services. They need to be aware of developing problems and not fail to exercise meaningful leadership in setting productive policy. Every board should assess its organization's operating environments, its organizational and individual competencies and develop strategies that enable them to assume leadership roles.

Recommendations

1. Start the process to reduce kill rates. If mass euthanasia of companion animals is to be reduced, the process must start in the board room. It will have to include a cohesive effort coordinating regional animal control programs, nonprofit animal organizations, regional veterinary associations, spay/neuter programs, kennel clubs and breeding organizations, government officials, dog trainers and behavior intervention programs, groomers, rescue groups and concerned volunteers. The educational effort must extend into the farthest reaches of the community. It is imperative that all animal professionals, especially veterinarians, be included.

2. Set a course for productive change in your communities. Boards must create a strategic plan to end the mistreatment and unwitting abuse of animals.

The biggest distinction between nonprofit humane societies and government animal control is that animal control agencies protect people from animals. Nonprofit animal organizations protect animals from people.

In assuming the traditional animal control role, most humane societies are besieged with direct care responsibilities and costs, rendering them ineffectual vehicles for education and prevention. Instead of creatively addressing the fundamental factors that fuel overpopulation, their resources are predominantly allocated toward collection and sheltering. These are crucial functions, but treating the effect at the expense of the cause only serves to perpetuate the vicious cycle. The central mission of any humane organization is to be on the front lines protecting animal life.
— Ed Duvin

3. Boards must be leaders and unite with other animal groups to form an area coalition. Include animal control, veterinarian, leading dog trainers, breed clubs, rescue groups and feral cat officials. Set regional goals.

4. Create shelter policy of longer care for impounded animals. This will increase volunteers, donations and adoptions.

5. Develop a formal strategic and operating plan that sets measurable goals, establishes objectives, provides action steps, designates the people responsible, create time lines and monitors results.

6. Commission a community animal survey to define the problem.

7. Renounce animal control contracts and direct resources to proactive animal protection and prevention programs.

8. Create programs to reduce animals in crisis, such as birth-rate reduction, owner retention and adoption programs to lessen the strain on animal control shelter capacity.

9. Create a headquarters for a feral cat TVAR program.

10. Develop plans for open cat rooms housing 12 to 15 cats per room. House dogs in spacious runs with other dogs, which reduces stress.

11. Initiate permanent identification programs.

Factor Two
Effective community organization and program coordination

Situation

As a result of animal tragedies, an ironic human tragedy unfolds. Shelter personnel see both the good and bad sides of people. They administer successful adoptions in which a loving bond is initiated. They witness joyful reunions of owners who temporarily lost their pets and they see the unselfish volunteer work of many caring people.[8]

Shelter employees also supervise the tragic rejections when an owner surrenders a pet for adoption because the bond never formed or has broken. They see animals daily whose time has run out and soon witness their demise. Each case is stressful, demanding individual attention and an attitude that must strike a balance between compassion and detachment.

Animal shelter personnel must deal every day with the emotional stress and conflict of killing large numbers of animals they are trying to help. For a century, the social value system has established that painless death for unwanted millions of animals is more humane than allowing them to suffer in a world that has no room for them.

The word euthanasia comes from the Greek words: *eu*, which means "good," and *thanatos*, which means "death." Webster defines euthanasia as "the act or practice of killing or permitting the death of hopelessly sick or injured individuals or domestic animals in a relatively painless way for reasons of mercy." This literal definition of euthanasia has been expanded by many shelters to include considerations for quality of life, space, health risks and fiscal limitations.[28]

Shelter culture defines the killing of animals as a humane act. Euthanasia is seen as a way to reduce animal suffering. As one worker observed, "I don't like any part of doing euthanasia, but I think it is more humane than letting them die on the streets. I'd rather kill them than see them suffer."

Death is seen as a preferable option to allowing animals to live under certain circumstances, even if they are healthy. For example, remaining in the shelter for a long time is viewed as worse than death for animals because they are confined in cages. The shelter setting is believed to be highly stressful to animals. Placing animals in bad homes, even though the animals would live, is also considered less acceptable than death.

To shelter workers, humane euthanasia refers to more than the purpose of death, it entails consideration for the animals' experience of dying. One worker noted, "We try to make it (euthanasia) loving."

Shelter workers have learned to shift moral responsibility for killing animals away from themselves to people outside the shelter who are seen as creating the necessity for euthanasia. The main targets of this shift are breeders who they perceive add to the pet population, negligent owners who create pet overpopulation by failing to spay or neuter animals and uncaring owners who surrender animals to the shelter for questionable reasons.

Workers adapt to the kill shelter by clinging to a sense of themselves as animal people engaged in a mission larger than merely killing animals. By seeing their acts as a type of crusade for animals and against an ignorant public, their killing is given moral, if not political meaning. By claiming for themselves the stance of combatants of pet overpopulation and providers of humane death, workers placed their killing in the category of euthanasia. No one liked or wanted to euthanize but everyone agreed that there was no other alternative to the situation they faced.

Attempts to clarify humane duties, as separate from animal control work, is unpopular with many animal control people who believe all shelters need to euthanize to properly maintain capacity. If shelters don't euthanize, they believe they are shirking their responsibilities.

Nonprofits have embraced this concept at the expense of sacrificing their moral credibility and depleting public support. By accepting this concept, nonprofit services have become indistinguishable to the general public from their animal control counterparts. The lack of public support weakens programs — programs that should expand the level of service provided by animal control — programs that keep next year's animals from becoming victims.

Admission Policies
There are primarily two kinds of admission policies: open and limited.

Open admission agencies accept all animals. Unfortunately, they must kill healthy, adoptable animals not claimed or adopted within a certain period to make room for new admissions. Frequently, killings occurs because the number of incoming animals are great and space is limited.

Limited admission agencies restrict intake of animals. They give animals more time to be adopted than the national average of three to five days. Many shelters that embrace limited admission policies are no-kill shelters, because

Open admission shelters are overwhelmed by a daily flood of animals that far exceed their capacity. Although this has given animal control a reason for being, it has also subjected them to the problematic details of caring for and housing millions of pets each year. Too often, the people who care most for the animals find themselves in the macabre position of killing animals.

We have to get consistency in what we are saying and doing. It is self-defeating when those who say we are protectors of animals continue to kill them when it isn't true euthanasia.

– Ed Duvin

they do not kill healthy, sound animals. No-kill shelters euthanize animals only when health or temperament warrant. They recognize the fact that they do not have the space to admit all pets brought to them and therefore it is necessary to turn away animals. No-kill shelters usually have long waiting lists of pet owners wishing to surrender their animals, knowing the animals will not be killed.

Animal control shelters are always open-admission agencies. Some non-profit shelters choose open admission policies. Open-admission shelters are overwhelmed by a daily flood of animals that far exceed their capacity. Although impounding animals has given animal control agencies a reason for being, the constant flow of animals has subjected them to the problematic details of caring for and housing millions of pets each year. Too often, the people who care most for the animals find themselves in the macabre position of killing animals. Simply put, when the volume of animals received exceeds kennel capacity, animals are killed. Space must be made to house new arrivals.

Animal Control Agencies

Animal control agencies have no choice in the matter of euthanasia. They are required to have open-admission policies and receive all animals — strays and owner-relinquished. If no homes can be found and the kennel space is near capacity, there is no alternative but to humanely euthanize unwanted pets.

Animal control does the hardest, dirtiest and most dangerous work. As long as man and animals live in close proximity to each other, conflicts will occur and there will be a need for animal control services. Animal control is the front-line custodian responsible for maintaining the animal-carrying capacity of the community. Animal control officers have, in effect, become urban game wardens.[7]

Virtually every community has an animal control program in one form or another. It can range from the local town policeman to established animal control agency with annual budgets in the millions of dollars. Certainly, it is essential for community governments to perform animal control. These agencies are mainly set up to protect public health and safety, manage animal-related complaints and problems, enforce animal regulations and protect the rights of citizens.

Additional responsibilities include the operation of community shelters that provide temporary food and refuge for orphaned dogs, cats and other domestic animals until they can be adopted or claimed by their owner. Their duties include pick up and reception of strays, response to incidences where animals have bitten or are vicious, and investigation of animal neglect and cruelty cases.

Most state laws require stray dogs to be held for a minimum number of days before they can be destroyed. City and county animal control shelters are usually funded with tax dollars. Their areas of responsibility can be divided by city and county jurisdictions. Many counties and some cities privatize their animal control operation by contracting out those services to humane societies and SPCAs. Government-operated agencies are usually responsible to the police department in smaller communities, health departments in larger communities, and some are responsible directly to an elected official. To a lesser degree, agencies can also be found under other governmental departments, such as waste management, zoning enforcement, human services, planning or highways.

The law gives government officials the authority to subsidize animal control programs. Tax money, along with license fees and other program revenues, fund animal control programs. The vast majority of homeless animals in any city or county is usually handled by an animal control agency.

The function of an animal control agency is to primarily protect the health and welfare of people in the community by impounding stray animals. They have legal power to enforce laws and animal control ordinances. They also patrol areas to pick up or receive surplus and stray animals that could cause automobile accidents, damage property or spread disease. They respond to citizen complaints and issue citations to pet owners found to be in violation of the law.

All too often these beleaguered agencies are under-funded and understaffed. Employees suffer from a hopeless resignation to the constant flood of incoming animals and the feeling of utter helplessness at ever correcting the problem. Consequently, many employees develop callous attitudes as a result of dealing daily with ignorant, abusive and irresponsible pet owners.

Available funding is limited and allocated to maintain day-to-day operations only. Funds are seldom available for proactive endeavors. Programs are judged by the number of citizen complaints received by the mayor's office, not how many animals are adopted, reclaimed or killed. No giant strides in zero population growth will ever come from municipal animal control agencies alone. The very nature of their funding and the allocation of their resources create a situation whereby they can only, at best, maintain the status quo.

Adoption programs vary. Some agencies believe they are just recycling their "problems" by adopting animals back into the community. As a whole, 6 out of 10 dogs, and 8 out of 10 cats that enter municipal shelters will be euthanized.

Some governmentally operated animal control agencies have a board of concerned citizens that assist in giving general direction to managers, allowing the community to have greater input into the activities of the program.

Nonprofit Organizations (humane societies & SPCAs)

Most communities are served by one or more private, nonprofit humane organizations. (SPCAs and humane societies are generic names that are used by many agencies across the country. Local humane societies are not nationally affiliated or controlled.) They have no membership rules, certification requirements or control by a national headquarters. Each agency is free to establish policies and procedures as they see fit. They function independently with their own board of directors, bylaws and policies as nonprofit corporations. These organizations will either be private shelters supported solely by public donations or private organizations that contract to provide animal control services.

People who work for government-managed shelters care about animals, and they should be the individuals who should be in the business of performing traditional animal control functions rather than SPCAs and humane societies. Humane societies should be on the front line educating the public and working to decrease animal control impoundment.

I believe there's a moral imperative for SPCAs and humane societies to say to their communities, in very direct terms, they will no longer kill healthy animals. Precious beings are not objects to be discarded at will, and this lamentable practice will continue until SPCAs and humane societies start expressing their outrage from the highest mountain tops. We desperately need community-outreach efforts that are commensurate with the magnitude of this tragedy, not more tiptoeing through the tulips. Hundreds of millions of healthy dogs and cats have been killed since Henry Bergh founded the first SPCA in the 1860s, and this slaughter will not end until humane societies and SPCAs, as well as the animal rights community, raise awareness.

— Ed Duvin

It is imperative that local nonprofit animal welfare organizations (humane societies and SPCAs) assume a leadership role in the war to stop the needless destruction of our nation's companion animals. Organizations must use their resources wisely and focus their work on proactive programs that protect animals from public abuse (either unwitting or blatant) as well as to augment government programs designed to manage public waste and maintain the carrying capacity of the community. They must work to unite all animal lovers in their community in a common cause to save companion animals from needless destruction.

The first step is to define the role of a nonprofit animal welfare organization. The focus of an active and productive community nonprofit animal welfare organization should be to protect the animals by working proactively to prevent tomorrow's distresses.

Their main goal is to reduce the volume of animals sent to animal control shelters by developing programs, both educational and functional that 1) reduce the birth rate of unwanted puppies and kittens, 2) keep animals in homes, preventing relinquishment and strengthening the human/animal bond and 3) providing high-volume adoptions. The ultimate goal is a good appreciative home for every companion animal.

Nonprofits must keep in mind the successful formula used by for-profit businesses: Give the public what it wants. San Francisco SPCA credits its success to "Doing what the public expects, and they respond." The public wants a nonprofit to be taking care of animals and adopting out animals. The public does not want a nonprofit to kill animals. The public spurns visiting an animal shelter when it perceives they will witness animals on "death row." The experience becomes too emotionally overwhelming. People let their animals loose on the street because they believe they have a better chance at life than taking the animal to a shelter. When public trust in the institution is eroded, citizens turn away.

The important goals needed are identifying services that people need to be successful, caring pet owners. Most people need counseling on acquiring a pet to align their expectations. Most people struggle with the decision to give up a pet. They need intervention to salvage the situation. If shelters have a negative perception, as most do, they will only use the services as ''a last resort.'' Shelter decision makers must get people to perceive them as a resource. They must work proactively to be an integral part of the community and help people reinforce the human/animal bond. Programs must be available to intervene when these relationships start to fail.

Private Shelters

Ideally, private shelters are proactive in their programs to solve pet overpopulation. They direct resources at the causes of pet overpopulation and work in areas of education, spay/neuter and adoption programs that augment the work of animal control. In concept, the idea is to prevent animals from reaching the crisis stage by developing programs that educate the community — programs that protect animals from direct or unwitting abuse. They also act to oversee government animal control agencies to ensure humane treatment.

Nonprofit organizations work to promote proper animal control funding and monitor activity to make sure resources are adequately used. The admission policy could be open, taking all animals, or limited, restricting admission because their shelter is full. Ideally the admission policy will be limited since euthanizing an adoptable animal to make room for an incoming animal is not in keeping with the humane ethic.

Most of these organizations provide programs that depend on the generosity of the community and the volunteers needed to staff them. Some humane organizations are able to offer adoptions; investigate reports of cruelty, abuse and neglect; perform spay/neuter surgery free or at reduced rates; give behavioral counseling; operate lost and found hot lines; conduct educational programs; administer pet-assisted therapy programs; give senior citizens free adoptions and provide property rental referrals to landlords who accept pets.

Some humane societies accept owner-relinquished dogs only on a space-available basis. Some take in strays. Generally, humane societies are more selective than government-run animal control agencies in screening potential adopters. All shelter adoption efforts focus on finding mutually compatible, long-term homes.

These charitable organizations are entirely dependent on private, tax-exempt donations like bequests and major gifts to fund their operations. As nonprofit organizations, they are responsible for raising funds, primarily through charitable donations to meet their operating expenses.

Humane societies & SPCAs with government contracts

Private nonprofit organizations such as humane societies and SPCAs don't serve themselves or their animal friends well by being in the animal control business. As protectors of animals, they have compromised their mission to keep animals out of harm's way. They have weakened their ability to prevent the future systematic destruction of these creatures, undermining their moral credibility.

Every dollar spent on proactive humane work that prevents animals from entering shelters saves seven animal control dollars. Birth-rate reduction programs, feral cat trapping programs, educational programs that strengthen the human/animal bond — these programs are more in keeping with the humane ethic. Organizations can't prevent abuse and protect animals when a majority of their budget goes to sheltering. That only serves to perpetuate the problem.

Local governments often contract with a humane society to enforce animal control laws and shelter impounded animals. There are several advantages for the municipality in this type of arrangement. The municipality is not usually required to invest up-front capital for a shelter, equipment and vehicles. This reduces program costs, ongoing payroll costs, as well as the number of complaints to city hall.

This arrangement necessitates the impoundment of all stray and unwanted animals into nonprofit shelters which are already overcrowded. When this happens, community shelter capacity (a critical resource) is cut in half. It also means impounded animals generally have on average, only three to five days to be adopted or claimed before being killed to make space for new arrivals.

[An] unintended consequence of non-profit animal welfare agencies practicing animal control is the diminished credibility and influence of so-called animal advocates because of the incongruity between their words and actions urging better treatment for animals while facilitating their destruction.

– Craig Bestrup

Households that turned over their dogs were approximately three times greater than the number of owners who allowed their dogs to breed, according to Gary Patronek, an epidemiologist specializing in pet-population dynamics.

The public perception is that shelters take in and care for all stray and homeless animals. In fact animal control shelters, on average, euthanize 60% of all dogs and 80% of all cats they impound. It is estimated that 20% of these animals are sick or aggressive and need to be euthanized. The remainder are euthanized to make space. This is not in keeping with the humane ethic.

Sometimes the nonprofit shelter only houses impounded animals. Animal control officers or the police departments handle field work. In other cases, a nonprofit agency may hire, train and supervise animal control officers. Nonprofit agencies collect fees from local governments for animal control service. They also seek private donations to support their programs.

Compelled by good intentions to help more animals and to provide direct service to the high numbers of unwanted pets, many humane societies find they have fallen into a trap. Kennel space is strained, euthanasia rates remain constant, volunteer recruitment and retention is difficult, and private donations diminish. These nonprofit agencies find they are caught in a public relations problem of being perceived as the ''bad guys'' and public support weakens.

The constant flood of needy animals drains resources to direct care costs. Agencies are remiss in not offering powerful proactive programs that protect animals from being victimized. This endless cycle of killing continues, unimpeded, with no one to prevent tomorrow's animals from becoming another statistic. Nonprofit agencies are caught in reactive management with little strategic planning and dwindling resources. Their only hope is that some rich person will die and "will" the organization a healthy bequest.

With government shelters, there is no choice. They must take all animals and euthanize the excess. Nonprofits have a choice. These shelters choose to take in all animals and, hence, kill. As a result, a large number of people who work at these facilities — people who want to work for the welfare of animals, who have an enormous amount of commitment, empathy and concern for animals — are compelled to kill animals. Their energy and skills could be directed toward prevention programs, which are much more beneficial to animals in the long run. Most of these people, like the animals they serve, are victimized, suffering burnout and other emotionally related problems.

Many nonprofit officials say they must step in because of the poor conditions at government facilities. Or they contend they must perform animal control functions because there is no other shelter. Nonprofits should become in as the primary shelter in the community. Rather, forces in the community should be brought to bear on politicians. Every community special interest group is trying to raid the community chest. That's the way the political system works in America. If groups don't represent companion animal interests, full funding for animal control will go to other community programs which have more vocal advocates and more of the costs for the care of animals will be shifted to the private sector. When a large group of people call insufficient service to the attention of government decision makers and rally public opinion, politicians will be forced to respond with the requisite service.

The government will be directed to perform professional service if a committee is organized to oversee animal control and shelter operations. Remember, there are over 100 million animal owners in America. Many of them are very influential.

No-Kill Shelters

Many nonprofit humane groups, realizing the moral duplicity of their predicament and frustrated with annual killing of thousands of healthy, sound adoptable animals, have initiated no-kill policies. The major distinction between no-kill shelters and traditional animal control shelters is the policy of long-term stay, which extends the average time an animal is in the shelter from the national average of under five days to however long it takes an animal to find a home (on average, 30 days). Consequently, adoptable animals are adopted, not killed. It just takes more time and effort.

These groups have decided to get back to their original mission of working to protect animals. They started applying their resources in proactive ways to supplement those of animal control. Their mission is to reduce the volume of animals admitted to animal control shelters and offer animals in their care more time to connect with new homes.

A common misunderstanding about the no-kill philosophy is that no-kills do not ever kill animals. Typically, shelters receive three categories of animals: 1) animals that are hopelessly beyond rehabilitation (about 25% of admits) like aggressive Rottweiler and feral cats with feline AIDS, 2) animals that are adoptable but are not desirable to the public or have minor illnesses, 3) highly adoptable animals (puppies, kittens, Persian cats, small dogs). It is necessary, in the truest sense of the word, to euthanize category 1 animals.

One organization that has stepped forward to lead the no-kill movement is Doing Things for Animals, of Sun City, Az. Under the leadership of Lynda Foro, this group promotes the growing no-kill philosophy movement through education, research and communication services. DTFA carries out its mission by providing services that include hosting the only national conference dedicated to finding humane and non-lethal solutions to the surplus animal population and by working with other organizations to prevent animal cruelty.

There are a growing number of no-kill humane organizations in the United States and Canada according to Lynda Foro. Ms. Foro says, "No-kill organizations expand the service base in communities."

In addition to aggressive marketing, which leads to high-volume adoptions, organizations offer educational programs, low-cost spay/neuter programs and clinics, pre-adoption counseling on pet care and ownership responsibilities, health care and rehabilitation programs for sick and injured animals, feral cat trapping programs, dog and cat training and crisis intervention programs, lost and found computer networked systems and pet-facilitated therapy. These programs are in keeping with the humane ethic.

Non sheltered Humane Groups

These very essential groups offer a variety of vital services like spay/neuter clinics, low-cost spay/neuter subsidies, rescues, referrals and adoptions. Many people work out of their homes and rescue animals in need. They also conduct education and community awareness programs. These people are the unsung heroes of the humane movement.

The no-kill community is often simplistically viewed by traditional animal control shelters as self-righteous individuals who thumb their noses at those working in traditional shelters. On the contrary, most no-kill activists have great compassion for traditional shelter workers, as they are victims, too. It's a question of fundamental principles, and those of us who believe in the sanctity of all life strive for a new ethic — an ethic that will end the needless killing of animals.
— Ed Duvin

Nonprofit Recommendations

1. See the "Model for Nonprofit Animal Services,"on page 44.

2. Renounce all animal control contracts.

3. Adopt a policy of long-term care for *all* animals admitted. Most animals will be adopted within a couple of weeks, though some may be there for three or four months. Ultimately, more animals will be adopted. It all depends on aggressive marketing of animals and connecting people with available pets. Animals may be euthanized for health or temperament, but it would be a small percentage. Volunteers, adoptions and donations will increase with this policy.

4. Design dog kennels and runs to house multiple dogs. New research indicates that keeping dogs in suitable packs can alleviate kennel stress and reduce barking. Cats do very well in open cat rooms. There are successful models that have used this configuration for many years. Kennel space should by modified to reduce stress and enhance adoptability.

5. Become the hub of all animal activity in the community.

6. Provide a resource center for people who want to acquire any pet, purebred or mixed breed, in the community. Network with responsible breeders to have a data bank of puppies available for adoption. By helping people acquire pets, humane societies and SPCAs will have the opportunity to educate a potential 87% more people than they currently reach.

7. Provide the largest dog training center in the community and network with all dog and cat trainers.

8. Say thank you and give appreciation to veterinarians who participate in low-cost spay/neuter programs by regularly listing participants in newsletters and local newspaper advertising.

9. Provide a dog and cat behavior-problem solving service that travels to people's homes.

10. Focus your goals on becoming a high-volume adoption center. Several studies have shown that the number of animals obtained from a shelter is a meager 13%. (The other 87% come primarily from friends, neighbors, "free-to-good-home" ads in the newspapers, pet shops and breeders.) Use marketing strategies that spotlight the wonderful animals you have available. Be aggressive. Work to create positive public perception and lure future adopters to your shelter. Use mobile adoption. It works. Keep in mind most people acquire an animal to improve their lives. Show them how their lives can be improved by adopting an animal from your shelter. You should strive for a 25% market share of dogs and cats acquired from all shelters in your community.

Model for Nonprofit Animal Services
Takes a proactive approach to reduce the volume of animals impounded by animal control

"Zero Population Growth"
Systems to monitor and control community pet population, taking into account the need for new puppies and kittens each year.

Birthrate Reduction
Feral Cat Spay/Neuter coordinate vet programs
Early age spay/neuter
Spay/neuter all shelter animals before adoption
Mobile Spay/Neuter Vouchers
Spay Day Events
Preseason kitten season promotions

New Dog Owners
Come to view shelter dogs or to get a referral to purebred litters available in the community. Receive new owner orientation and dog training certificate

NONPROFIT ORGANIZATIONS
Main mission: Protect Community Animals and Prevent as many as possible from harm
Goal: Zero population growth
Goal: 100% Spay/Neuter Rate for owners who are not "professional breeders"
Goal: A Spay/Neuter Clinic and Voucher Program
Goal: 100% (free) ID for community animals
Goal: New owner orientation & training programs
Goal: High volume adoptions of shelter animals (25% Market Share)
Goal: 100% Pre-Adoption Spay/Neuter
Goal: Lost and Found Networked Computer Program with 50% Return to Owner Rate
Program: Owner Orientation w/ Mandatory Attendance
Program: Feral Cat Trapping (TTVAR) Headquarters
Program: Crisis Intervention — Behavior Problem Solving
Program: Media Events to increase demand for animals
Program: Rental Housing
Program: Orphaned Animal Medical Care and Rehabilitation
Policy: Long-term stay for all sheltered animals
Program & Policy: Coordinated activities and shared goals with animal control; receive transferred animals, help manage adoption and lost and found programs.

New Cat Owners
come to shelter to get healthy, spay/neutered kitten or cat. Receive education on cat care.

Increase Adoptions
Administer adoption program at animal control
AC Transfers
Adoption Outreach
Positive shelter appearance
Animal Behaviorist
Foster Care
Adoption Pluses-
Health Guarantee, Grooming, Microchip, Visual ID, free class, leash or carrier
Fund for medical care to treat sick and injured animals

Fun Pet Events
Dog obedience trials
Cat shows
Dog walks
Agility training
Dog Parks for exercise
Halloween dress-ups

TRAINING
New Owner Orientations Puppy Training &
Dog Training Classes
Dog & Cat Behavior Problem Solving
Crisis Intervention

New Pet Acquisition Service & Counseling
Help People attain a pet (use an off-site business location) Matching service between pets available and wanted.

Citizen Oversight Committee of Animal Control Programs w/ leadership from non-profits

Government Animal Control
Mission: Protect the Citizens from Animals through legislation and law enforcement
Duties: Impound Stray Animals, Respond to Complaints, Issue Licenses, Give Citations, Conduct Rabies Clinics, Return Lost Animals to Owners, Conduct Cruelty Investigations, Adopt Animals, Educate the Public.

43

Humane societies in America should be driving the dialog. They should be leading their fellow citizens and not just involved in the day-to-day crisis management of a shelter.

11. Become partners with animal control "cousins." Focus your goals on community entry and exit numbers. Augment animal control programs by assisting or taking over their adoption, lost and found, and cruelty investigation programs. Develop a system where you become an adoption-only service. All strays go to animal control. Nonprofit shelters take in owner relinquished animals only. In addition, nonprofits receive animals transferred from animal control as space allows.

12. Become a feral cat trapping (TVAR) headquarters.

13. Make humane education the main thrust of all animal welfare efforts. Pet owner irresponsibility, lack of commitment, behavior problems and failure to spay/neuter are all root problems that need to be addressed through aggressive community humane education programs.

14. Humane education means more than letting grade school children pet the animals. Teacher curricula should be an integral part of all humane education programs, but resources should be directed at the immediate problem of uneducated owners. A large portion of dogs and cats are relinquished because of an owner's failure to solve minor behavior problems. Many people forgo training because of cost or an inability to recognize their lack of knowledge and skills. The public should take a test that would determine their level of understanding and, if they fail, alert them of the need or formal training.

15. Work to change the behavior of irresponsible pet owners who constitute one of the main problems. The animals are not to blame but unfortunately, they are inadvertently punished.

16. Conduct all-out birth-rate reduction programs, such as spay/neuter clinics, voucher programs, feral fix or "casually owned" spay/neuter programs. Include the animal control shelter in your program to sterilize all animals before release.

17. Avoid strict adoption screening practices that are counterproductive to your goals. Sometimes there will be borderline adopters, give weight to veterinary references. Use "quality control" follow-up systems to ensure suitable placements of questionable adopters.

Photo by Jana De Peyer

Animal Control Recommendations

1. Animal control services should be funded from revenues raised by a per capita fee of at least $5 per person. These fees will fund spay/neuter subsidies and underwrite microchipping programs. Additionally, per-capita revenues will allow waiving impoundment fees for first-time, low-income offenders. It is appropriate the entire community shares the financial burden of animal control. Similar to the costs of maintaining police and fire departments, animal control is used by the entire community and their main activities benefit their health and safety.

2. Network with other organizations in the community to coordinate programs and responsibilities.

3. Share goals. Examine regional statistics, not agency statistics. Look to reduce the *combined* entry and exit numbers of animals in your region.

4. Recognize we all have a role in a common battle, not against an "animal problem," but a "people problem."

5. Cooperate with nonprofit organizations. Animal control is the ultimate depository for orphaned animals. Any effort to keep an animal from impoundment is positive. The main thrust behind any shelter is aggressive adoptions, not housing animals forever.

6. Transfer animals to other organizations. Use purebred and mixed breed rescue groups. Give them the benefit of the doubt until they prove otherwise. Give them a break on fees. These groups are your allies.

7. Have nonprofit animal organizations assist with the marketing of animals for adoption. Seek a combined market share of 35%.

8. Since it's the behavior of pet owners that must be changed, tailor animal control officers' interactions with pet owners to encourage responsible pet ownership. Coercing owners with threats and punishment is counterproductive.

9. Share data bases. Exchange information on lost and found animals, people who have been found guilty of abuse and people who relinquish animals. Share lists of animals up for adoption for possible match with people looking for a certain animal.

10. Join forces and exchange information on cruelty investigations.

11. Develop veterinary programs. Work together to develop low-cost spay/neuter clinics and a voucher system.

12. Spay/neuter 100% of released animals. Immediately enact shelter policies to ensure all adopted animals are altered prior to release.

Organizing a Community Coalition

Community animal related organization need to work together with one common goal — To Save and Protect Animals. The community coalition concept involves an alliance of animal related organizations to save the largest number of animals by working on and improving the system.

Typically, animal related organizations are caught "putting out fires." Lowering kill rates in regions requires improving the system and dealing with causes and the process which create the crisis so as to prevent them in the first place. Several steps are necessary to accomplish this mission:

1. Develop a mission statement and a name.

2. Develop common goal(s) such as; lowering area impoundment, lowering the average age a cat or dog is spay/neutered, lowering euthanasia rates, increasing adoptions, increasing veterinarian participation, developing low-cost dog training classes, crisis hotlines, etc.

3. Identify resources and capabilities and the role of each participating organization and their limitations. i.e. animal control, humane society or SPCA, all breed dog rescue, feral cat trappers, trainers and behaviorists, AKC dog all-breed club, pure bred rescue, groomer rep, Cat Fanciers' Assoc. representative, spay/neuter organization(s) and local veterinarian association representative.

4. Everyone must agree to respect the limitations and the services provided by each organization.

5. Identify opportunities for improvement.

6. Create a climate where honest dialogue can begin. Communication should be direct and honest, with respect for others and full disclosure to all. Avoid labeling, keep an open mind and agree not to talk negatively about other organizations.

7. Agree on a central information source to take data in and distribute it out to members and the media.

8. Initiate a community-wide pet survey. Collect and analyze data and use conclusions to solve problems. Be objective. Decisions must be based on facts. "In God we trust but all others must use data" applies here.

9. Refer to organizations best suited to respond to the need.

10. Cooperate with adoption transfer programs.

11. Provide quality animal care for all animals handled.

12. Work toward building consensus and accomplishing objectives. Keep the discussion focused on facts, objectives and action steps to accomplish goals. Then measure your progress.

13. The 85-15 Rule of Total Quality Management applies. This rule states that eighty-five percent of all work place problems are management problems that are in the system, the way the work gets done. Improvements to the system should be planned (analysis of data), worked, checked and based on the results either systematized or re-planned for success.

Community coalitions can eliminate duplication of services and save everyone money. They address the questions, how can we work smarter and, how can we improve working together? Moreover they can create a productive, cost-effective service delivery system for the good of companion animals.

Community coalitions are recommended by the California Council of Companion Animal Advocates, the Duffield Foundation and have been promoted for years by Karen Medicus of The Humane Society of Austin and Travis County, Texas

Factor Three

Proper data collection, scientific assessment of information, strategic planning and coordinated action based on findings

A problem cannot be solved unless it is first defined.

Situation

A problem cannot be solved unless it is first defined. There is currently very little objective data to accurately estimate the extent of animals dying needlessly in shelters. Although animal shelters are responsible for the overwhelming portion of euthanasia performed for population control, they are not always required to make public or even to maintain records of animal intake and disposition. There is no national agency that regulates animal shelters operated by private nonprofit groups or regional county or city governments.

The first step in determining the most effective strategies for reducing the number of pets euthanized will depend on systematic collection of animal shelter data and population-based surveys of pet ownership, acquisition patterns and reproductive status in each community. Without such knowledge, it is difficult to plan community programs and shelter operations or to monitor and evaluate actions aimed at reducing the tragic numbers of unwanted dogs and cats. Obtaining accurate information about the numbers of animals handled and the numbers euthanized in shelters is further confounded by a lack of uniformity in methods used for the collection and reporting of data from shelters and humane societies.[33,42]

To date, there have been few attempts to determine how successful efforts have been or to identify the most important factors responsible for pet overpopulation, pet roaming, relinquishment and abandonment in local communities.

Although billions of dollars have been spent on dog-population control programs, little attention has been devoted to program evaluation. The lack of accurate and relevant data has impeded critical evaluation of program performance, and it remains unknown which factors were responsible for the substantial decrease in euthanasia that has occurred since the late seventies.

The few studies of community pet populations have revealed that certain factors play important roles in population dynamics. These factors include birth, death, migration, population structure of pets and human demographics. Although the pet population structure and its interaction with human demographics can be complex, a simple, realistic model can be simulated.

A community pet population structure is basically composed of four subpopulations: household (owned), roaming (stray), feral, and shelter pets. These subpopulations constantly interact to form a connecting network. Although it is sometimes difficult to make a clear distinction, a roaming animal is one that has an owner or a home to which it returns and a feral animal is one that is homeless and unowned.

Nonprofit animal shelters and organizations are at the epicenter of activity and play a key role in structuring the forces to combat pet population.

Conducting a Community Pet Population Study

The Steps to Conduct a Study[32]

1. Identify the scope of the inquiry.
2. Prepare the questionnaire, using an expert.
3. Determine the number of surveys to be sent.
4. Randomize the sample.
5. Prepare the mailing:
   Address the envelope,
   enclose the questionnaire, self-addressed return envelope, letter of introduction.
6. Edit the returned questionnaires and determine a format for entry into a computer.
7. Follow up on non-respondents.
8. Enter information contained in the questionnaire into a computer.
9. Analyze the data.
10. Prepare the report.
11. Identify practice decisions.

Key Information Needed on Pet Population

- Number of owned dogs and cats in the community
- Population ratio; i.e. dogs per persons, cats per persons percent of dogs and cats spayed or neutered
- Breed of pets
- Source of pets including percent migration
- Spay/neuter data (yes/no, any litters before)
- Original cost of acquiring the pet, age of pet at time it was acquired, pet age distribution within the community
- Distribution of dog population as to size (small, medium, or large dogs)
- Birth rate
- Length of ownership and fate of previously owned pet
- Number of pets disposed of or died in past three years and method of disposal
- Average number of pets per pet-owning household

Shelter

- Percent of population entering the shelter
- Percent of population roaming
- Percent and means of disposal of shelter population
- Source of animals entering shelter
- Type, size, age, sex, etc. of shelter population
- Projected shelter population
- Demographic data relative to persons redeeming, adopting or relinquishing a pet

Animal Health and Economics

- Type or place of pet housing
- Type of food
- Exercise methods
- Percent of animal behavior problems
- Average number of visits per household to a veterinarian
- Average expenditures per household for veterinary services
- Type of veterinary services sought

Human Attitudes

- Reasons for not spaying or neutering
- Reasons for disposing of pets
- Disadvantages of pet ownership
- Attitudes toward confinement
- Attitude toward pet ownership

Household Related Data

- Percent pet ownership (dogs, cats, or dogs and cats)
- Household make-up including ages and number of humans, race, religious affiliation, type of housing
- Effect of income on pet ownership
- Member of household responsible for pet care
- Occupation of income producers
- Employment status
- Effect of housing type on pet ownership
- Percent of households planning to acquire a new dog or cat
- Percent of households prohibited pet ownership
- Do they feed stray cats or kittens?
- Would they adopt a pet from an animal shelter?

Leading organizations like the Massachusetts SPCA have outlined strategies aimed at reducing the number of pets relinquished to the MSPCA's shelter system based on data from local surveys and from the shelter system in which the strategies will be implemented. It is critical to focus efforts to conserve limited resources. Monitor the results of strategies that have been implemented. If data reveals that a strategy is effective, consideration can be given to expansion of that program. On the other hand, if the desired result is not being attained, the strategy must be modified or abandoned. Clearly, an effective data-collection system is crucial to the development of focused strategies and to the monitoring of program effectiveness. (Karen Johnson consults in these types of studies, (408) 363-0700.)

Recommendation

Organize a study of pet population dynamics. A comprehensive community study is best undertaken as a joint effort by groups concerned with animal welfare, pet populations, pet health and pet ownership. Humane societies, veterinarians, municipal animal control departments and shelter operations will all find components of an appropriately designed study that will have a direct bearing on their professional planning and day-to-day management decisions. Individual veterinarians can undertake a somewhat more limited study, but careful planning is necessary if this effort is to be worthwhile.

Factor Four
Comprehensive, community spay/neuter programs

Situation

Ovariohysterectomy (spaying) in female and orchiectomy (neuter) in male animals are the mainstays in the war to reach zero-population growth.[14] The pet population has been sizably reduced since the early 1970s when spay/neuter was aggressively promoted by animal welfare advocates. The clear advantage in the surgical option is that irreversible infertility is attained immediately.

In the early 1970s when the pet overpopulation peaked, low-cost sterilization programs were not well received by the veterinary establishment. Representatives at the 1974 American Veterinary Medical conference argued there was no need for special spay/neuter programs since a low-cost and effective chemisterilant was imminent.[42] Twenty-four years later we have yet to see such results.

The issue is money. Veterinarians, as business people, need to be paid a fair price to perform sterilization surgery. Most pet owners think the price is too high. Animal welfare organizations are caught in the middle, trying to talk veterinarians into participating in low-cost programs while trying to remove the obstacles that prevent people from spaying/neutering their pets.

The 1970s and 1980s saw the establishment of many low-cost spay/neuter programs and clinics. These clinics and programs are sponsored by animal welfare organization and a source of concern and controversy to private practitioners.[48]

A Massachusetts SPCA survey found the major influence to spay or neuter came from previous experience (58%), animal-advocate groups (33%) and veterinarians (29%), a surprisingly low amount.

Veterinarians at low-cost spay/neuter clinics perform surgeries on animals owned by low-income or needy community residents although 10% of the clientele could afford to pay full cost. These clinics are often perceived by the public as inferior to higher caliber veterinary clinics. Low-cost spay/neuter clinics are mostly used by clientele that veterinarians would not normally see.

Low-cost spay/neuter clinics have not had a negative effect on overall veterinary income which continues to rise. The practice of spay/neuter, however, is not considered a major profit procedure for participating veterinarians. Full retail price is charged to clients who do not declare a financial need, which allows veterinarians to break even when they discount spay/neuter services.

Animals that are spayed and neutered cannot add to the problem of overpopulation. Surveys have revealed that people need low-cost programs. Surveys also reveal the vast majority of people (70%) want to be responsible by sterilizing their pets to prevent unwanted pregnancies, roaming, to settle the animal down and to prevent fights.

The spay/neutering of dogs and cats has to be increased and must include every animal not designated for breeding.

Some may be reluctant to alter their dogs because of close psychological extension with their pets. Reasons for owners balking at "fixing" their pets are historical and cultural, including a person's attitude towards birth control in general and religious beliefs.[23]

Cat owners are more likely (80%) to have their pet spay/neutered than are dog owners (53%). The leading reasons for not having the animal spay/neutered were different for cat owners than dog owners. [18]

Dog owners said they confined the dog and prevented roaming (30%), they wanted to breed the dog (25.3%), and some blatantly said they saw no need (16.9%). Cat owners said the cat was too young (37.5%), they saw no need (24.2%) and the cat was not allowed to roam (12.5%). About 11% of cat owners stated the procedure was too expensive.[24]

There are persuasive arguments for spay/neutering. Spay surgery keeps roaming males away from the house. Neutering reduces the risk of roaming and fights, provides health benefits to the pet and makes the pet friendlier and less aggressive.

Data presented in a study of Iowa and Washington indicates a good portion of all female dogs (79%) are spayed, although the proportion is likely to be lower (50%) for dogs less than three years of age and higher (80%) for dogs over 3 years old, which results in an overall rate of 69% (Teclaw et al. 1992).

Only 2.8% of dog-owning households in Washington and Iowa whelped in 1991. These dogs represented 18.7% of the reproductive pool and only 1.8% of the total dog population.[36]

When a high percentage of the dog and cat population is sterilized, unwanted litters can still be a problem. The current sterilization status of a female is not a reliable indicator of her lifetime reproductive performance. The lifetime rate of litter production among sterilized females is close to that of intact females. About 20% of owners are allowing their animals to have at least one litter before sterilization. This can account for a significant supply of animals.

The problem with spay/neuter as a means of birth control is that it is:

1. Costly surgery requiring a licensed veterinarian.

2. Complications do occur, although risks are slight, from anesthesia, incision dehiscence, and postoperative infections.

3. Based on religious orientation, there are many Southern European and Latin nationalities who object to birth control for pets.

Cat owners are more likely (80%) to have their pet spayed or neutered than are dog owners (63%).

Recommendations

1. Spay/neuter contracts in which owners sign an agreement and pay a good faith deposit to have their pet altered are not an effective way to guarantee sterilization compliance. These pets add to the problem.

   Shelters must not release intact animals. A study of one shelter found as many as 20% of the animals adopted from the shelter had a litter. This is unconscionable. Seven states have mandated that spay/neuter deposits be collected for pets adopted from animal shelter. The deposits are refunded on proof of surgery. These laws are not effective as many people forego the deposit and pets go unaltered despite the financial incentive. Shelters keep the money. What does that accomplish? Professional animal shelters spay or neuter animals before they leave the shelter. This should be the law. It's a more costly approach for shelters but obviously a more effective one.

2. Maintain an ongoing educational program featuring a campaign on overpopulation and responsible animal ownership. People must be reached who have obtained animals from sources other than shelters. Veterinarians must play a lead role. People must be educated, persuaded and often financially subsidized to spay/neuter. Educational programs must target the realities that people don't know that cats can have litters as early as four months. Early spay/neuter benefits must be uniformly pushed.

3. Create a regional goal of lowering the age a pet is spay/neutered. The goal is 4 months/no litters. This will raise community awareness.

4. Increase the availability of low-cost sterilization surgery with low-cost clinics, vouchers, government subsidies and participation in spay-a-thons events. Make it economical for people who feed wandering cats to have them altered

5. Use "Spaymobiles." They work. Animal Matters in Westbrook, Connecticut, performed 8,200 sterilizations and vaccinations in 1997 in its mobile unit.

6. Work to institute differential license fees that favor spayed and neutered dogs and cats; they have proven to work if the gap is not too big.

7. Distribute scientific findings on early age spay/neuter to all veterinarians with the intent of having them strongly recommend to clients the spay/neutering of their pet before four months or their first estrus.

8. Do more research on sterilization pills that produce antibodies that block sperm from fertilizing the egg.

9. Lobby for more cooperation and subsidization from government sources. Perhaps the most successful cooperative effort between animal shelters, veterinarians and health departments is a model program in New Jersey. Participating veterinarians throughout the state perform the surgery for 80% of their regular fee and are paid from a user fund. There should be increased lobbying efforts to have states contribute funding so that veterinarians don't provide their services at a loss and can aggressively promote spay/neuter.

10. Promote early age spaying and neutering as the norm, promoted by all breeders and pet stores.

A study by Peter Theran, DVM, titled *Early-age Neutering of Dogs and Cats*, published in the March 15, 1993, Journal of the American Veterinary Medical Association concluded, "Neutering can be performed safely in 6-to-14-week-old dogs and cats. Furthermore, after the surgery department became accustomed to slightly different instruments and procedures, neonatal neutering was performed as efficiently as was the same surgery on older animals.

The reports are conclusive, early-age spay/neuter is not harmful. Veterinarians need to understand this procedure will save animal lives.

Factor Five
Permanent identification programs

Situation

Almost three quarters of all animals coming into California animal control shelters are strays. If not claimed by owners or adopted, they are killed. These animals have a tremendous impact on precious space and human resources. Strays represent a significant portion of the problem.

Animal control programs receive a portion of their funding from dog (and sometimes cat) license fees. Not only do programs receive license fees, but they also profit from impoundment fees that owners have to pay to reclaim their dogs. Currently, government animal control programs have a vested interest in supporting dog licenses with identification tags as a means of returning dogs to owners. Unfortunately, the current system does not work. A new permanent pet identification program that is administered on a local level with local and national databases is needed.

The best way for owners to ensure the return of lost animals is to keep them tagged, with phone numbers and addresses included on the tags. In theory, dog licensing programs are meant to force owners to ID their pets. Animal control authorities issue fines for noncompliance.

The majority of owners fail to license their dogs. Most programs show only a one-third compliance rate. Current licensing programs have not proved an effective means of returning lost dogs home. Nationally, only 14% of dogs and 2% of cats that enter shelters are returned to owners.

Almost three quarters of all animals coming into California animal control shelters are strays. Current licensing programs have not proved an effective means of returning these lost dogs to their homes.

Organizations must embark on an all-out campaign to put microchip identification on pets at 4 months of age and, if necessary, subsidize the cost. In the long run, microchipping will substantially reduce the needless killing of cats and dogs by returning lost pets home. It also will provide a means to track owner and breeder behavior.

Visual identification should augment microchips. When visual identification (dog tags) are used with a phone number, many good Samaritans find stray animals, secure the animal and call the owners. The animals are returned home without impacting overcrowded shelters.

Once an animal is lost, many owners do not search for it immediately. Some may not start their search for days, thinking and hoping the animal will find its way home. For those who do search, there are many reasons why lost or stray animals may not be found and reclaimed. Legal stray holding periods, ranging from three to five days, present a very short time period for a successful search. Many owners who let their animals roam don't start seriously looking until after three days. Animals can roam large areas and numerous shelters could be harboring them.

Recommendations

1. Governments should promote microchips by offering reduced or free license rates. For example, if a license cost $15, owners would receive four free years or a free lifetime license. Animal control would receive revenues for services rendered and know where to go to collect. Initially, governments must be willing to fund animal control from the general fund. Over time, less animals will be received, reducing costs.

2. Technology should be expanded to include more information on the chip itself, such as pedigree, breeder, registration, owner, vet etc.

2. Issue local animal control licenses with the owner's telephone number used as the registration number.

3. Where there are license programs featuring phone numbers on the tag as the registration number, non profits should assist animal control in making an all-out effort to promote licenses. Publicity campaigns should be used along with other compliance measures.

4. Elevate the importance of visual identification programs. Visual identification returns the dog home without impacting the space at shelters. Free ID programs with a request for donations have proven to be successful. Most people donate more than the cost of the ID.

5. Use computers for quick searches on a number of characteristics to improve the possibility of an over-the-phone search being successful. Computers can help us increase our ability to match phoned-in reports of animals lost with phoned-in reports of animals found.

6. Form computer networks to link the records of all animal shelters in the area onto one database for easy access by the public, vet hospitals and pet stores.

Feral cat colonies have an ecological niche. If an established colony is removed for any reason, another will migrate into the vacated territory, usually because of the availability of food.

Feral cat numbers fluctuate between 40 and 60% more than the owned cat population.

Factor Six
Programs to deal with the uncontrolled reproduction of feral cats

Situation

It is estimated there are approximately 40 to 60 million feral cats living outdoors throughout America. Feral cats are wild and shun human contact. They are very adaptable, which allows a large portion of them to survive in the wild. These cats are prolific reproducers. The availability of food and absence of real threats from predators, compounded with early sexual maturity and multiple yearly births, make feral cats a problem of epidemic proportions.

To a large extent, the problem of feral cats as the primary origin of cat overpopulation is overlooked. A 1975 study by Schneider and Vaida pointed out "the problem of overpopulation is more acute in the more fertile feline population than that of the canine population."

Feral cats can be found living virtually anywhere, in cities, suburbs, beaches, college campuses and rural areas across the United States. Their survival shows the same patterns as wildlife, with seasonal ups and downs. According to a study by *Animal People*, feral cat populations range from 26 million in January, to 40 million in June. Their numbers fluctuate between 40% and 60% of the owned cat population.

Most of these cats have been wild for generations. A few show signs of once being owned; they may have strayed or been abandoned. Nevertheless, they are easily reintroduced to households. Kittens under eight weeks of age are easily socialized and domesticated, however once a kitten reaches two to three months of age, domestication is difficult.

A New Zealand study of feral cats by Langham and Porter revealed the density of cats correlated with the availability and dispersion of resources. Where food is abundant and den sites are common, high densities have been recorded, from 200 to 2,300 cats per colony. High urban densities develop because a cat's diet consists of plentiful garbage or refuse, often supplemented by pet food. In rural environments, where they have to catch a portion of their food, cats are less abundant and their numbers probably reflect prey density. The mean density on farmland range from 1 to 20 cats per farm.

Feral cat colonies have an ecological niche. If an established colony is removed for any reason, another will migrate into the vacated territory, usually because of the availability of food in the area. As long as there is a constant source of stray felines, as is currently the case in the U.S., another colony will form. Trap and kill programs have proven unsuccessful because they have ignored this fact.

Detractors say feral cats feed on birds and are the culprits for dwindling bird populations. They cite the potential for the transference of disease to trappers. They also question the ability to properly maintain colonies over time.

Alley Cat Allies (ACA), the group responsible for developing the National Feral Cat Network, is concerned that efforts to vilify cats could result in misguided attempts to exterminate feral cats. The reduction in some species of songbirds has many concerned people looking for answers about who or what is to blame. A campaign recently launched by The Humane Society of the United States and the American Bird Conservancy erroneously targets all free-roaming cats, including managed feral cat colonies, as the "problem."

"Studies indicate that cats are not the primary culprit in dwindling bird populations," says Becky Robinson, co-founder of Alley Cat Allies (ACA). "The World Watch Institute and other environmental research groups verify that the decline of bird and other wildlife populations is directly linked to the loss of natural habitat. Urban sprawl, tropical deforestation, the construction of shopping malls, roads and golf courses and increases in pesticide use and pollution are to blame. We need to put constraints on our own behavior, not the normal processes of nature."

A significant number of scientific studies conducted on the diets of feral cats indicate their impact on bird populations is negligible. These studies conclude that cats are rodent specialists, with birds comprising only a small portion of their diet, and that cats can prey on bird populations on large land masses without destroying these populations. Cats are opportunistic feeders and often live primarily off of rodents, garbage and handouts from humans.

As noted by B.M. Fitzgerald, a long-time researcher of feral cats, "Birds in suburban and rural parts of Britain have co-existed with cats for hundreds of generations. Any bird populations on the continents that could not withstand these levels of predation from cats and other predators would have disappeared long ago."

Since its founding in 1990, Alley Cat Allies has practiced and promoted the control of feral cat populations using non-lethal means, including the trap-alter-release method successfully employed for decades in countries such as England, South Africa and Denmark. They coordinate activities nationwide and can be reached by calling (202) 667-3630 or visit them on the Internet.

Methods of Dealing with Free-roaming Cats

Trap and Kill

Several tried approaches exist to manage roaming cat populations. The preferred method of animal control organizations has been to capture and euthanize unowned, roaming cats.

Animal welfare advocates consider trap-and-kill methods inhumane and objectionable on several fronts. The chief objection is that it is ineffective. It has been proven as soon as a cat is removed, a new one will move in, assuming a steady food source is available. Another objection to trap and kill (more humane and moral) is that, unless a cat is making a threat to human welfare or is causing unusual harm, it is worthy of life, even though it does not have a human address.

Trap/Vaccinate/ Alter/ /Release/Maintain (TVARM) Program

A typical TVARM program works very simply and methodically. An advanced reservation is secured at a participating spay/neuter agency by the feral cat caretaker. Traps are obtained with a small deposit. Cats are trapped using written instructions for humane treatment. The traps are always monitored so

A New Zealand study of feral cats by Langham and Porter revealed the density of cats was correlated with the availability and dispersion of resources. Where food is abundant and den sites are common, high densities have been recorded, from 200 to 2,300 cats. High urban densities develop because a cat's diet consists of plentiful garbage or refuse, often supplemented by pet food.

Trap-alter-release method of feral cat management has been successfully employed in countries such as England, South Africa and Denmark for decades.

Photo by Jana De Peyer

the cats do not spend a long time in them. The cat is taken to the spay/neuter agency where it is surgically altered. Minor cuts, abscesses, and parasites are also often treated. The cat's ear is notched for identification and monitoring and returned to the person who is maintaining the colony. The cat is then released back into its originating environment, providing it is a safe one. The colonies are managed by continued trapping and altering.

Kittens are removed from the colonies and scheduled for adoption. They are tested for FeLV and FIV. Normally, 5% of feral cats are found to have FeLV and 2% are found to have FIV.

Many leading organization such as Alley Cat Allies, Feral Cat Coalition and Operation Catnip have stopped testing all feral cats for FeLV and FIV. They found that of $16 spent, $11 was spent on testing. Because they found the infection rate low, they were spending about $200 to identify each positive cat. They concluded a far bigger benefit to the welfare of feral cats was to use precious funds to sterilize more cats.

Feral Cat Coalition (FCC) of San Diego, California proclaims a 50% reduction in cat impoundments in San Diego County shelters since 1992, the year it began operation. Its statistics reveal the following: of the 3,153 cats trapped and altered, 54% were female, 46% were male. Of the 1,639 females trapped, the following characteristics were noted: 1) only 3% were found to have been already altered, 2) 17 cats were refused surgery for being under five months of age, or too ill, 3) 18 cats died during surgery, 4) medical treatment was needed for 679 cats (22%), generally antibiotic and anti-parasitic medications. Cleaning and suturing of wounds and abscesses was also very common.

Of these stray females, 72% were either in heat, pregnant or had recently delivered kittens. This is at least a three and a half times higher rate of pregnancy than found among owned cats.

For the FCC program, veterinarians donated their services and supplies were purchased through donations. However, the cost of these services and supplies would average about $52 per cat in a low-cost clinic. Looking at the figures from San Diego, for a cost of $163,956 (3,153 cats x $52/cat), the shelter numbers have dropped by at least 6,500 cats. The average three-day stay for a cat in a California shelter is estimated at $70 per cat. By reducing the number of cats handled by 6,500, San Diego saved $455,000 over a two-year span. This successful track record indicates no additional funds need be raised. The program will pay for itself through lower shelter costs. Additional funding for altering could be taken from the shelter budget.

Following TVARM programs, mating behavior and noise associated with breeding are eliminated. The male urine spray smell is eliminated.

The human health risk of rabies is often touted as a concern in the management of roaming cats. In California the risk is very slight. There has never been a recorded case of a human acquiring rabies from a cat in the state's history. Only two cases of cat rabies were found in 1993 in the entire state of California out of a current population of some 10 million owned and stray cats. Skunks, bats, and rodents are more of a rabies threat.

In 1989, Stanford University officials announced a plan to trap and kill approximately 500 stray felines living on campus. In response, Stanford Cat Network (SCN) was formed. SCN was able to present an alternative solution to stop the progression of cat reproduction on campus. They proposed and organized a TVARM program.

Because of SCN's work, Stanford cats' now have zero population growth and the population is declining through natural attrition. Over 60 kittens were caught, socialized and adopted during the first season. By 1994, only four kittens were found on campus. The population is now estimated at approximately 300 cats. Stanford's current cat population is healthy and well-cared for. Its maintenance involves students, staff, and faculty.

SCN has accomplished all of this without financial support from the university. SCN's successful five-year program with a very large cat population demonstrates that feral cat colonies can be managed and kept under control. Workable, viable alternatives to extermination do exist.

Issuing vouchers for residents to take their stray and "loosely owned" neighborhood cats in for free altering is another successful method.

Veterinarians have control over whether or not they will alter the feral feline. If an animal is too sick or has other problems, the practitioner can decline to do the surgery. Attached to the voucher is a short, anonymous questionnaire for the owner to complete. This form, which is returned to the department handling the program, asks ownership questions useful to monitoring its success and to determine who is using it.

In San Jose, Calif., the reports have been positive. Veterinarians have experienced no problems, the people redeeming the vouchers like the program. Results after three years showed that ferals constituted 40% of the surgeries, 61% were female, 16% were pregnant. The number of cat intakes in San Jose shelters dropped 10% while surrounding cities, which have no voucher program, have only decreased 1%. The $30,000 spent by the county on the program has saved the taxpayers $100,000 in sheltering costs.

The San Francisco SPCA also has an active, successful, free altering program. Any feral feline brought to the shelter is altered free of charge year round. Owned cats are altered for a low-cost most of the year and free during May, June and July. Starting in 1995, SF SPCA also started paying a $5 "bounty."

The dog's domestication began 12,000 years ago, whereas taming cats was attempted much later, around 3,500 years ago, in Egypt

Critical Concern

The management of the feral cat crisis is a major problem for animal control and a paramount challenge for humane animal welfare organizations. Animal control organization are not structured to address this problem. If progress is to be made, it must come from nonprofit animal welfare organizations.

Recommendations

1. Initiate Trap, Vaccinate, Alter and Release programs, the most effective method for stabilizing and reducing feral cat populations. Conversely, animal control programs to remove and exterminate are ineffective, costly, frequently inhumane and publicly unpopular.

2. Recognize veterinarians who cooperate by listing their names with special thank you notices in newspapers. Create a special plaque for their office waiting rooms. Cooperative veterinarians, who have a skilled staff to properly handle ferals, are crucial. In addition to sterilization, healthy cats will need rabies vaccinations and medical examinations.

3. Implement innovative, progressive and aggressive grassroots efforts to solve the overpopulation of feral cats with coordinated volunteer activities and veterinary services. Public support is critical. Programs should include high-volume, low-cost spay/neuter clinics, vouchers for low-cost service at veterinary clinics, mobile veterinary vans and spay/neuter marathons before kitten season..

4. Develop communication campaigns that strongly urge people who feed cats they do not own to act responsibly and sterilize the cats. Low-cost clinics and voucher programs must be in place to assist these efforts.

5. Start a mobile spay/neuter van strictly for cats that is coordinated with feral cat trapping efforts.

Factor Seven
Pet Retention

Situation

A misconception among those who believed that sterilization alone would decrease euthanasia rates was that "unwanted" births resulted in pups and kittens flooding into shelters. Most animals in shelters are not, in fact, young pups and kittens, but rather "adolescents," approximately 6 to 18 months old, which have outgrown their cuteness and are manifesting minor behavioral problems their owners have neither the skills nor patience to resolve.

Municipal and private shelters became inundated with the steady flow of castoffs the public no longer wants. What should have been a lifelong commitment, for some, turns out to be 4 to 6 months.

Companion animals live with us and share our homes and lives. When the relationship works, it's beautiful; when it doesn't, there is always the pound or humane society to deal with the problem.

The majority of animals that are relinquished by their owners and subsequently euthanized are products of broken bonds — relationships that failed to mature or were severed for frivolous reasons like lack of planning, lack of patience or failure to meet the owner's expectation.

Most people get a pet with the best of intentions. They have visions of the ideal dog or cat from childhood, from a neighbor or friend, or television. Few, as Plato says, "do evil knowingly" — most people are ignorant of simple animal behavior.

Only one-third of all dogs and cats remain in their original household for their entire life.

58

It is not surprising that a certain segment of the population makes little effort to locate lost pets. In fact, these people are relieved to be rid of a problem. Most thought they had a dumb or stupid dog. "There is no such thing as a bad dog, only uninformed owners," a wise dog trainer once said. Unacceptable behaviors, including inappropriate elimination and the male tendency to roam, are frequently cited as the reasons an animal is no longer in a home.

Surprisingly, many owners expressed guilt or regrets about surrendering animals to the shelter; 58.8% said they would keep the pet if the problem at hand could be resolved.[37]

Over 50% of animals in shelters are classified as strays because they have no identification. No conclusive evidence has determined if these animals were intentionally "dumped" or if they wandered away from home. However, 60 to 75% of them show evidence of being owned. The percentage of a city's roaming canine population varies from 4% to 10%, suggesting that the problem is originating from a small percentage of pet owners.

The most frequent age for relinquishment was less than one year old. Approximately 35% were no longer in the household at one year of age and more than half of the loss was because the pups were no longer wanted. Those surrendered to animal shelters were approximately 33% of the total loss. "Households that turned over their dog were approximately three times greater than the number of owners who allowed their dogs to breed."[37]

Pet owners are varied and have multiple views of ownership. On the one hand, pets are taken into the home and showered with affection, some spoiled beyond belief. People consider their pets to be part of the family. They sleep on their owner's beds and they eat premium quality food. Bonding is strong. Owners receive true companionship and their lives are enriched while pets receive a home, food and tender loving care.

Other people value pets for their uniqueness or their potential economic value. Still others want to possess animals but do not feel a strong sense of commitment or emotional connection to the animal. They fail to develop the human-animal bond. They feed the animal out of obligation with slight interaction. Veterinary care is minimal. Containment is with a chain or a pen in the backyard or animals are left to roam the neighborhood at will. Identification and license registration is regarded as unnecessary. When the female becomes pregnant and has a litter, the puppies or kittens are advertised in the local newspaper. Some are placed, the remainder are taken to the local shelter.

The typical "unwanted dog" had been acquired free, probably from a friend or neighbor, or had been born at home. It had been selected to provide companionship or company for the children (71.9%). It was surrendered because of changes in the owner's lifestyle (27.7%), behavior problems (26.4%), or the fact that its care required too much time or responsibility (11.6%). One of these factors made the animal expendable, a trip to the shelter expedient and the "last resort."

The typical unwanted cat comes from the stray or feral population and was found by a good Samaritan who attempted to care for it but eventually brought it to the shelter.

Those who do not retain a pet are more likely to be first-time adopters, have children in the house, be males, be younger than those who kept their pets, and more likely to have obtained their pet "for the children."

"Traditional solutions to pet overpopulation, such as sterilization, and newer initiatives, such as laws designed to discourage or prohibit breeding have attacked the problem from the supply side of the equation (breeding) and appear to discount the role of consumer demand and pet retention in the pet overpopulation equation. The effectiveness of supply-focused interventions has been questioned. There is a growing body of evidence that euthanasia reduction efforts must also focus on the demand portion of the pet population equation. This implies that irresponsible pet acquisition and ownership is a primary cause of pet abandonment and euthanasia."
— Gary Patronek

A major study of pet relinquishment was conducted in Alamada and Contra Costa counties in California.[46] A follow-up survey was done one year after to determine what happened to the animals in the initial survey.[47] Approximately 12,000 households were contacted in the follow-up survey. Adopted pets leaving households for any reason constituted approximately 15% of the canine population and 25% of the feline population. Of these losses, approximately 40% of dogs and 30% of cats were given away by their owners.

Another prominent study found the median period in a household for an adopted pup that left during its first year of life was 4.4 months. Assuming the average pup entered the household at six weeks to two months of age, the median age at which pups were disposed of would be approximately seven months, which agreed with the age pattern of dogs found in shelters.[37]

Sadly, *only* one-third of all dogs and cats remain in the original household for their entire life.[43]

Raising a pet is much harder in the 1990s than in previous decades. Forty years ago, the pet-care scene was different. A typical household in the 1950s consisted of a family unit in which the wife was at home all day. She raised the children, took care of the family dog and was responsible for housebreaking and training the dog. This household typically had a small, fenced-in yard.

The living environment has changed drastically. Because of property restrictions, many homes of the 1980s and 1990s are not allowed to have fenced-in yards, making it difficult to keep a dog outside. In addition, apartments and condominiums where pets are accepted are scarce.

Furthermore, human-pet daily interaction has decreased. As a culture, we find it far easier to expend money rather than time with our pets. Because of the economic conditions of the 1980s and 1990s, families in which husband and wife work are common, leaving pets home alone all day. Although dogs have pent-up energy, owners are tired when they come home from work and often cannot exercise or play with the pet. Even if the owner is at home, other interests often interfere with daily interactions and the pet's need for exercise. It's no wonder some dogs, primarily larger breeds, take to roaming.

Owners may not know that certain inappropriate behaviors can be corrected or prevented by proper training, understanding, and recognition of the animal's natural behavior. Consequently, euthanasia for behavior problems is a major cause of pet deaths. Vast numbers of pet owners have no knowledge of training animals and work on folk misinformation ("Rub his nose in it if he messes in the house,") or absurdities (Beat or reprimand the dog for not coming when he finally does come.) On the other hand, others spoil and anthropomorphize animals to extreme.[41]

Many pet owners believe that an animal simply cannot adapt to a new owner and therefore demand euthanasia if they cannot keep it. Others truly believe surrendered animals will all be placed in good homes by humane societies, not knowing that most will be killed. Many animal owners have no idea of the personalities, physical or psychological temperaments associated with the breed of dog they own.

Many people are to blame for their lack of preparation before choosing a pet. There are many resources available on pet care and animal behavior, yet many obtain an animal with little regard for temperament. Veterinarians, as a whole, have been lax in their own animal behavior education and fail to adequately respond to owner needs. What owners learn are often old wives' tales and half-truths, like "A dog is happy kept outdoors in a big backyard." (A dog is happiest when its' with it's pack.)

Some perpetuate ownership patterns and myths handed down from parents to children. Some owners, often from rural or agriculture backgrounds, see companion animals as livestock and peripheral to their homes and lives. Others, who are often from urban lifestyles, see the acquisition of certain animals as status symbols or extensions of their personalities and an image they wish to project.[27]

In too many cases, owners fail to recognize the commitment they are about to undertake. When the stray wanders in, when a child brings home an adorable puppy or kitten, or when the trip is made to the breeder or home advertising pets in the newspaper, many are caught in the moment. Many of these animals, which are acquired haphazardly and impulsively, despite the best of intentions, are readily sacrificed when conditions of ownership change. They become modular pets, to be plugged in and out of the families' lifestyles.

When the situation grows tiresome, the animal is "dumped," sometimes in the country where it may die of starvation or be hit by a motorist. Sometimes they are passed off to a friend or neighbor who quickly tires of the impulsive decision to help out. The animal often winds up at an animal shelter, where, because of overcrowding, its odds of surviving are slim.

Recommendations

1. Develop a system to identify at-risk owners, then provide the requisite training. Testing systems are used for drivers, marine-boat operators, gun owners, etc. If we truly value an animal's life, we should make sure that deficiencies in knowledge of animal care and training are identified and that systems are in place that offer proper education and instruction.

2. Since training systems are imperative, bring together a coalition of shelters, veterinary hospitals and clinics, pet supply stores and dog/cat trainers and behaviorists. Organize a network that will provide new owners with a free group orientation session by a qualified behaviorist. Extensive training programs should be scheduled and coordinated.

3. Provide training for low-income families at a nominal cost. Space should be available in classes for hardship cases.

4. Develop special programs for behavior problems. Weekly workshops should be scheduled on such topics as chewing, barking, digging, house-soiling, cat scratching and roaming. Use crisis hotlines.

"There is no such thing as a bad dog, only uninformed owners."
Barbara Woodhouse

Eighty-four percent of the public want a dog or cat under one year of age. If demand for puppies and kittens remains unchanged without an increase in public demand for adults animals (over one year of age), shelters will continue to kill large numbers of adult dogs and cats.

Factor Eight
Balance of Supply versus Demand

Situation

Currently, there are major supply/demand imbalances that drastically affect animals in shelters and lead to massive killing of pets.

Some 84% of the public want a dog or cat under one year of age. If demand for puppies and kittens remains unchanged without an increase in public demand for adult animals (over one year of age), shelters will continue to kill large numbers of adult dogs and cats.

If the supply of puppies is reduced from one particular source, that is, responsible breeders, the supply from other sources (backyard, fast-buck breeders) will rise to meet that demand, without proper buyer education.

Only 12% of cats and 13% of dogs are obtained at shelters. Currently, shelters have very little effect on community animal-acquisition dynamics. Any for-profit marketing manager would be up in arms at such a small market share when the product offered has so many benefits to the acquirer.

People are partial to purebreds which constitute 55% of all dogs. This preference has not changed and probably will continue.

A Las Vegas study found 52% of the dogs in shelters were large breeds, compared to 35% of the general pet population.[31] People want small dogs. The majority of dogs killed in shelters are medium to large dogs. In addition, people are partial to light-colored dogs. Black and mixed colors are not favored.

Over half of the available metropolitan housing market is rentals, and of these, most rental units have "no pets allowed" regulations or strict regulations prohibiting dogs over a certain height. There is high demand and not enough supply for "pets-allowed" housing. Very few professional property managers will accept pets.

A large number of cats come to the shelter during kitten season, which extends from March to September. Good Samaritans sometimes find homes for these kittens, but most are taken to the shelter. The supply of kittens is so high, compared with the demand, that shelters can place only a small percentage.

During economic hardships, more pets are relinquished. Fewer pups and kittens go to homes and fewer lost animals are reclaimed by owners from pounds and shelters.

According to Gary Patronek, traditional solutions to pet overpopulation (like sterilization) and newer initiatives (like laws designed to discourage or prohibit breeding) have attacked the problem from the supply side of the equation (breeding) and appear to discount the role of consumer demand and pet retention in the pet overpopulation equation. The effectiveness of supply-focused interventions has been questioned. There is a growing body of evidence that euthanasia reduction efforts must also focus on the demand portion of the pet population equation. This implies that irresponsible pet acquisition and ownership is a primary cause of pet abandonment and euthanasia."

Recommendations

1. Promote a better public image of shelter animals. The public must perceive these animals as life enhancing. Make efforts to change the stereotype of the poorly behaved or sick dog/cat.

2. Feature older dogs and cats. Testimonials should be used from happy owners. Display pictures in your community of kindly adult dogs.

3. Instigate feral-fix programs well before kitten season.

4. Measure adoption programs against normal market share (13%). Shelters should employ aggressive marketing techniques similar to those used by North Shore Animal League in Port Washington, NY, which uses display ads, fliers, yellow pages, special promotions and media events. Then animals are adopted more quickly so that most stay in the shelter for only three to four days. (If it works there, it can work for you if done right.)

5. Obviously, the theme of "Come on down and adopt an animal before we kill it," is not working. Shelters must continuously work to improve how they display animals, reduce smells, consult with prospects, provide tours with an adoption counselor. They also must hold media events that feature the positive aspects of acquisition to change the image of shelter animals. Adoption outreach can be used at pet stores, vet offices, major employers, and shopping malls.

Factor Nine

High-volume shelter adoption programs

Situation

The most challenging aspect of addressing pet overpopulation lies in reaching and effecting change in people who have no contact with animal shelters. Shelters do a poor job of recycling animals back into the community. According to a National Pet Food survey, 13% of dogs and 12% of cats are obtained from shelters — an appallingly small percentage.[18] Why?

Shelters have a large number of wonderful animals available. Yet, most are killed because no one wants them. Anyone who has worked in a shelter for a period of time knows how great these animals are. Has the shelter community inadvertently turned people off by promoting a message of death? Does the average person become depressed at the thought of seeing all those faces on "death row" and decide to avoid a trip to the shelter? Do shelters open their doors and expect people to walk in without any promotion?

Shelters must learn to compete in the marketplace. To some, that thought is repugnant. "This isn't a business; we're here to save animal lives," some may retort. How wrong that is! Can you imagine forprofit businesses not marketing their products. There will always be sources other than animal shelters for obtaining pets.

Experts estimate that every year 12% of the animal population turns over, dies, and is replaced by new puppies and kittens. The object is not to create more homes for pets by persuading people who would not otherwise have got-

"Veterinarians are usually good sources of information concerning the physical anatomy, requirements, interests, and needs of the animal. Yet when it comes to the mind of the animal, the psychological and behavioral aspects of the animals' telos, the veterinarian too often is lacking. It is very unlikely that the veterinarian has had a single course in animal behavior, behavioral pathology, and training, yet the lives of pet animals often depend upon the veterinarian's ability to successfully resolve problems like a pet who house-soils, a pet who destroys furniture or a pet who strays."

— Bernard Rollin

ten a pet to get one (called growing the market), but to persuade people who would otherwise get a pet from some other source to adopt it from the shelter (market share).

Recommendations

1. Increase market share by becoming more aggressive about promoting shelter animals. First, examine all the dynamics that go into a decision to obtain an animal and create your marketing programs accordingly. For instance, people want healthy animals, so you offer health guarantees. Do people know they get an animal that is temperament tested, vaccinated, altered, identified and comes with free health checks by participating veterinarians?

2. Use advertising and public relations effectively. People lead busy lives and don't know what you've got until you tell them. Don't sit back and expect people to walk in the door. In the shelter business, time doesn't mean money — it means life.

3. Increase market share by elevating the status and attractability of shelter animals. Groom the animals and improve the look of your shelter with bright, happy colors. Keep cute photos on display.

4. Promote adoptable animals inexpensively through public-service announcements, free advertising and special events such as adopt-a-thons.

Factor Ten
Curtail amateur and backyard breeding

Situation
To best understand the dynamics of breeding, it is important to look at the situation in terms of zero-population growth. This concept recognizes the yearly consumer demand for new animals and the historical popularity of pedigreed dogs and cats. It gives recognition to the need for responsible breeding by people who adhere to ethical standards.

Pedigreed Cat Breeders

The Cat Fanciers Association has been leaders in efforts to promote the well-being of all cats. They have sponsored not-for-breeding registration, show classes for altered cats, public service announcements and educational programs. The CFA has issued grants for the study of feline heath and the dynamics surrounding "pet overpopulation."

Pedigreed cats represent only 3% of the total cat population in the United States. In 1997, 19,873 breeders registered litters with the Cat Fanciers' Association (CFA), the world's largest registry of purebred cats. An average litter is estimated at between three and four kittens. In an average year 85% of breeders have one to four litters, 14% have five to twenty litters and 1% produce 21 litters or more.

Approximately 65,183 pedigreed kittens were registered in 1997. In contrast, the total U.S. household yearly demand for kittens is estimated at well over 7 million, with most of the kittens coming from feral colonies.

The CFA pioneered the not-for-breeding registration that is used for pet-quality kittens born that do not meet the breed standard. Over 50% of kittens born do not meet standards and are sold as pets. The buyer signs a contract stating the kittens will be altered and the owner cannot register any offspring.

The CFA has been a leader in efforts to promote the well-being of *all* cats. They have sponsored not-for-breeding registration, show classes for altered cats, public-service announcements and educational programs. The CFA has issued grants for the study of feline heath and "pet overpopulation." It also allows altered pedigreed cats and random-breed cats at its exhibitions to "showcase their beauty and individuality."

Most pedigreed cats are loved and valued, and there are large waiting lists for kittens. These cats are highly domesticated, confined indoors and cherished members of the household. They do not pose an animal control problem. Pedigreed cat breeders and members of CFA are not part of the problem.

Pedigreed Dog Breeders

The American Kennel Club (AKC) records from 1986 to 1997 show the number of AKC registered dogs to be between 1.3 and 1.5 million annually. The number of litters have remained around 550,000 since the start of the decade. Of the top 25 breeds, seven are large: Labrador Retriever, Rottweiler, German Shepherd, Golden Retriever, Boxer, Siberian Husky and Dalmatian. The 1990's have seen significant change in the public desire for larger dogs.

An estimated 6,360,000 dogs are born annually in the United States in 4.9% of the dog-owning households. Of those dogs 2,925,600 (46%) are mixed breed or accidental births. The remaining 3,434,400 or 54% are purebred. Of those pure breeds, 1,333,568 or 39% are registered with AKC and 2,101,863 (1.6% of dog households) or 61% are unregistered.

One of the myths of pet overpopulation is the assumption that AKC puppies are bred by breeders and sold in pet shops. Statistics reveal that only 5.7% of all AKC-registered puppies are sold in pet shops. In truth, 90% of puppies sold in pet shops come from commercial breeding operations.

Of AKC registered dogs, 67% never have a litter, 22% have one or two litters in their lifetime, and 11% have three or more. Only 10% of registered dogs compete in AKC events.

The American Kennel Club is not part of the problem. Animal activists argue these breedings take up a home that a shelter dog could have and contribute to the problem. The fault with that logic does not take into consideration public demand. People have historically desired purebred dogs so strongly that purebreds account for 55% of the dog population. This will not change until there is an increased demand for mixed breed dogs.

The American Kennel Club offers a number of educational programs to promote responsible dog ownership and owner-dog bonding. They recently invested 7 million dollars in DNA technology that will assure the accuracy of the registry and weed-out fraudulent registrations. It's alarming to think where the dog community would be without AKC-affiliated dog-training programs. They have provided a forum for knowledge and competition, inspiring many owners to a better relationships with their dogs.

In a 1993 survey of 15,000 people, the question was asked, "What organization is best at giving advice about the care and training of dogs?" Respondents rated AKC as best (36%), followed by the ASPCA (26%).[17]

1997 Cat Fanciers' Association Top 10 Registrations	
1. Persian	39,114
2. Maine Coon	4,819
3. Siamese	2,657
4. Abyssinian	2,308
5. Exotic	2,037
6. Oriental	1,337
7. Scottish Fold	1,202
8. American Shorthair	1,072
9. Birman	1007
10. Burmese	939

An estimated 6,360,000 dogs are born annually in the United States in 4.9% of the dog-owning households.

1997 AKC Dog Top 20 Registrations

1. Labrador Retriever
2. Rottweiler
3. German Shepherd Dog
4. Golden Retriever
5. Poodle
6. Beagle
7. Dachshund
8. Cocker Spaniel
9. Yorkshire Terrier
10. Pomeranian
11. Shih Tzu
12. Chihuahua
13. Boxer
14. Miniature Schnauzer
15. Shetland Sheepdog
16. Siberian Husky
17. Dalmatian
18. Miniature Pinscher
19. Pug
20. Boston Terrier

Different Types of Breeding

Purebred animals are under represented in shelters. About 20% of dogs (very few puppies) and less than 3% of cats enter shelters. A much smaller percentage are killed. Many purebred dogs come to shelters as young adults.

One solution to pet overpopulation was aimed at creating laws designed to discourage or prohibit breeding. This simplistic approach caused more harm than good. It targeted the role of the supplier (breeders) and discounted the role of demand (owner) and the pet-retention factor. A high percentage of dogs are being destroyed because of behavioral problems, which include house-breaking problems, hyperactivity, continuous barking, and destructive habits. If behavioral problems were eliminated and shelters affiliated with purebred rescue groups, the killing of purebred dogs in shelters would be minimal.

To understand the problem associated with breeding it is important to understand the different types of breeders.[15]

Hobby Breeders-Exhibitors

These individuals are actively involved in a breed and usually belong to a breed club. Concerned about improving the quality of their breeds through selective breeding, they retain the best stock for their breeding programs, then present the animals for appraisal in the show ring. They sell "pet-quality" puppies and kittens to the public and "show-quality" to other show breeders.

They raise the offspring with an abundance of human contact, have clean kennels, use health screening to prevent genetic defects and screen potential adopters to make sure every animal placed has a good home. A true fancier of the breed, most of these breeders subscribe to ethical guidelines which includes a tenet to take back a pet that is orphaned should the pet need to be relinquished.

Some of these breeders are more concerned about conformation than temperament. They do not properly educate new owners and many do not strongly recommend spay/neuter or early-age spay/neuter surgery, which contributes indirectly to unwanted pets.

Show breeders belong to national registries. The two biggest national registries are the American Kennel Club (AKC) for dogs and the Cat Fanciers' Association (CFA). National dog and cat registries such as the AKC and CFA maintain pedigrees and register purebred dogs and cats for recognized breeds. The AKC recognizes 145 breeds of dogs, and the CFA 39 breeds of cats. AKC licenses approximately 4,000 clubs in the United States and the CFA more than 600 clubs.

National purebred organizations are very concerned about animal welfare issues and promote responsible pet ownership. The AKC has been a leader in dog training and has created standards by which all training is measured. It also encourages responsible pet ownership through the development of such programs as the Canine Good Citizenship Test. This test raises public awareness about the responsibilities of pet ownership and being considerate of your neighbors while promoting the benefits of having a well-behaved pet.

Obedience clubs promote dog training, and their member/trainers volunteer in communities across the United States to help new owners learn how to become better pet owners. Many of these clubs sponsor public classes, from basic "house manners" and "puppy kindergarten" through advanced obedience, for nominal fees that are just enough to pay for the building rental (Members seldom receive any compensation.) Since animals are often abandoned because of behavioral problems, the positive impact that these clubs have on the surplus animal problem is substantial.

The CFA and AKC print excellent educational brochures on the importance of sterilizing pets and on other animal welfare topics such as information on the care and feeding of particular breeds, responsible pet ownership practices, such as spaying and neutering, licensing, confining, identifying, and training. They also publish informational magazines.

All-breed dog clubs provide educational workshops for dog fanciers and the public. Dog and cat shows offer educational booth space to other nonprofit animal charities, and cat clubs allow humane societies to bring cats to their shows for adoption.

Most of these clubs have purebred rescue committees whose efforts account for a major share of purebred rescues. After rescuing animals from shelters, members are responsible for following through with shelter adoption policies, including spaying and neutering. In some areas, where shelter budgets are low, kennel clubs maintain special rescue funds for sterilization and rehabilitation. Thousands of rescue clubs are available nationally.

National breed clubs strongly urge their members to issue spaying/neutering contracts with every sale of pet-quality pups. National clubs started providing such contracts for their members, and soon the use of such contracts became standard practice. The AKC created a limited form of registration for non breeding, pet-quality pups.

Pedigreed dogs constitute approximately 55% of dogs in America, mixed breed 45%..

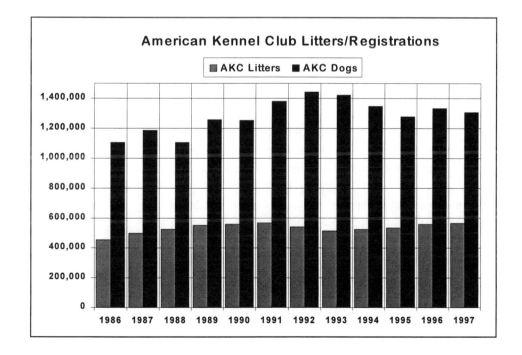

Commercial breeders

These individuals breed pets for profit. They work to maintain quality and pay attention to good genetic practices that will produce healthy animals. They have acceptable physical facilities, sanitation and nutrition. Their breeding stock is, most often, average. Many commercial breeders use veterinary care. Preventive health screening for genetic diseases are seldom used. This breeder sells pups through breed magazines, brokers, pet stores and private parties. Often these breeders are not particular enough about to whom they sell and could do better at socializing their pups.[15]

"Just one litter" breeders

They usually own one dog and breed "just one litter" for the following reasons: 1) they want extra money, 2) they want another dog that is an off-spring of the bitch, 3) they think their dog is beautiful and want to have a litter, 4) they want the children to be involved in raising a litter of pups and 5) they heard that bitches need to have a litter of pups before being spayed.

The scenario goes like this: a family has a Labrador Retriever bitch it purchased from a breeder and their neighbor has a male. The family breeds the dogs in hopes of recouping their initial cost of obtaining the Lab and making some extra easy money. The reasons given by pet owners for breeding their pets are not generally endorsed by reputable breeders. They are viewed as frivolous or irresponsible.

Typically, "Just one litter breeders" are ignorant and irresponsible about animal welfare problems. They operate alone, without club affiliations through which they learn genetics, health certifications and ethical guidelines. In most cases, these breeders incur more costs than anticipated, experience more work in caring for the litter than anticipated, give little forethought to finding suitable homes and experience trouble placing the litter. Half of the litter will be sold through newspapers. After the puppies chew up the living-room carpet, some are given to friends or relatives (of which a portion will end-up at shelters), and some will go directly to a shelter. Some of the puppy owners will repeat the cycle. These breeders are contributors to the overpopulation problem.

Puppy Mills

Puppy mills are dirty, dingy places where one or several popular dog breeds are kept in overcrowded conditions, constantly reproducing to provide income for the breeder. These litters produce ill-tempered puppies that are prone to health problems. The sire and dames daily needs are barely met. These puppies are wholesaled to an ignorant public through brokers or sold directly to consumers through newspapers with little regard for placement criteria. Unwitting buyers are eager to obtain a pet, usually at a lower price.

Many low-income people propagate popular breeds of dogs in run-down conditions with limited knowledge of proper breeding practices. They often refrain from veterinary care because of cost. Puppy-mills are primarily in rural areas of the Midwest although every community has some.

The term "puppy mill" is tossed about with little regard for accuracy. It is often used to define anyone who breeds pedigreed animals or the origin of all puppies in a pet store. Unfortunately, good, reputable, conscience breeders are accused of being puppy mills.

Puppy mill conditions were a major driving force in the passage of the Animal Welfare Act (AWA). The U. S. Department of Agriculture, who is responsible for enforcement of the act, administers the AWA. This agency oversees the proper distribution and handling of animals. They license more than 4600 animal dealers and they are responsible for issuing licenses to breeders upon satisfactory inspection of kennel facilities.

If you believe there is a puppy mill in your area, make sure you get your facts straight before you act. Contact purebred rescue, your local animal control, humane society and the U.S. Dept. of Agriculture in Annapolis, Md. for further investigation and law enforcement.

Recommendations

1. Ensure those involved in breeding of pedigree dogs and cats recognize their responsibility, adopt into permanent homes, educate owners on the importance of spay/neuter and they are always *available to take back a pet when and if necessary.*

2. Recognize responsible breeders. People want purebred dogs and cats. Public demand for purebred dogs and cats will change only slightly from year to year. Zero population growth strategy recognizes the value of breeding in order to preserve desirable and predictable physical and temperamental characteristics and satisfy public demand.

3. A local certification system should be established that recognizes and supports responsible breeders and weeds out undesirable practices. Policing should be done from within local breed groups and be organized similar to real estate boards that censure and discipline unethical agent practices. Certified, responsible breeders who conform to ethical standards should be supported, not vilified.

4. Develop a local referral service and receive back substantiated reports from new owners, veterinarians and groomers on owner satisfaction and breeder responsibility (similar to the way the Better Business Bureau works). The problem is not responsible breeders. The nation needs more certified, responsible breeders. The problem stems mainly from accidental breeders and amateur, backyard charlatans out to make a quick buck on the sale of puppies.

5. Establish a permanent identification of all AKC-registered pups. You cannot control the problem if you cannot identify it. Microchip identification is available, safe and inexpensive. All licensed breeders should implant microchips in their pups. Microchip technology should have information such as breeder's name, address, owner's name, national breeder number, veterinarian and pedigree.

A major study of relinquishment factors related to dogs and cats was conducted by the National Council on Pet Population (Salman et. el. 1998). Results from exit interviews with 3,772 former owners who relinquished their animals revealed only 4% of relinquished dogs were enrolled in a dog training class, 1% had a private lesson and 1% sent their dog to a professional trainer.

Persian cats are by far America's favorite. In 1997, 39,114 Persian cats were registered. The second most popular cat, the Maine Coon, registered 4,819.

6. Develop a community pet-acquisition counseling and referral service. This would be composed of a network of shelters, veterinarians, breeders and kennels. Callers would be directed to responsible breeders only. Shelters would have the opportunity to educate future pet owners on breed temperament, health care and behavior problem-solving.

7. Use dog training and socialization programs to help clients train their new pups and avoid behavioral problems before the crisis stage. Veterinarians, humane groups and dog trainers should be included.

8. Convince veterinarians that their influence is needed for early age spaying/neutering programs for pet-quality kittens and puppies.

9. Increase limited registration. The AKC has a vehicle in place for breeders to register their pups as non-breeding dogs. Breeders need to start using this program, enforce spay/neuter contracts and strongly recommend early-age spay/neuter.

10. Work to abolish breeding with total concern for aesthetic standards, which results in perpetual genetic defects and does not consider a dog's natural physical ability or temperament.

11. Enforce breeding ethics. Target backyard, amateur and accidental breeders who operate outside the system. Communities should identify and eliminate all disreputable breeders and practices. This includes inadequate facilities, substandard or no sanitation, substandard nutrition, genetically inferior breeding stock, no records or breeding plans, inhumane treatment and no preventive health program.

12. Laws that focus on supply-side intervention to curtail breeding do not work. They always involve tampering with the free-market system, a sacred cow in America. It would be more productive to influence demand by educating future owners on responsible breeding practices and directing those individuals to accredited breeders. Involve local breed clubs in the accreditation of breeders.

13. Require pet stores to spay/neuter puppies before the owner takes possession. Sell puppies with limited registration. Pet stores could also act as an outlet for adoption of unwanted pups and kittens from local humane groups.

14. Accredit commercial breeders. The mission of breed clubs and national kennel clubs should be to offer national and local certification programs that give reputable breeders the opportunity to distinguish themselves from charlatans, with poor breeding standards, who cast aspersions on the breeding avocation. Such facilities would meet ethical standards. Principals would be trained in companion-animal husbandry. AKC limited registration would be aggressively used. Many of the pups would be spayed or neutered prior to sale.

15. Veterinarians should be driving the dialogue. The pet-owning public looks to the veterinary profession for leadership in the health and welfare of its animals. While veterinarians have accomplished much in advancing animal health, unfortunately, they have let others take over animal welfare and need to take a more active role.

16. Allow mixed breed dogs to participate in obedience competition. The AKC should embrace the training needs of all dogs as the Cat Fanciers' Association allows for altered pedigreed cats and random-bred cats at their show.

Factor Eleven
Programs to care for sick and injured animals

Situation
The chances of survival for homeless, sick cats or dogs in shelters are slim. Medical treatment is costly, space is tight, and most people don't want to adopt sick animals. Care and rehabilitation take time, space and money.

Because of limited space and financial resources, animal control shelters have difficulty rehabilitating sick and injured animals. It's a different story for nonprofit organizations. In an article titled "The Role of Animal Shelters," in *Animals' Agenda*, Diane Allevato, executive director of Marin Humane Society, posed a rhetorical question: "What would you do if you were confronted with a cat with three broken legs and you only had $1,000?" [4]

It seems Allevato answered her own question several months later when the agency announced the establishment of a new intensive care facility for cats. A local philanthropist read the article and donated funds to underwrite the program. A cat named Jack reaped the rewards. He showed up with a broken jaw and a battered body. After several weeks of treatment and loving care, he was adopted to a good home.

This is a good example of the role of a humane society. It must establish the program, then solicit donations to fund the program. As the message goes from the movie *Field of Dreams*, "Build it and they will come!" Experts advise that future fund-raising success will depend on how well nonprofits can communicate programs, as well as their efficiency and effectiveness. These programs are more in keeping with the humane ethic.

A study of the euthanasia of cats performed by the National Pet Alliance revealed 44% of cats at the Humane Society of Santa Clara Valley in California were euthanized due to sick and poor health condition, 20% were euthanized because they were feral and 18% because they were too young. These categories accounted for 82% of cat euthanasias. The majority of illnesses are minor problems like upper-respiratory infection (cat cold) and kennel cough.

A National Pet Alliance study of cats revealed 44% of cats at the Humane Society of Santa Clara Valley in California were euthanized due to sick and poor health condition, 20% were euthanized because they were feral and 18% because they were too young.

Shelters must do more than exhort about guardian responsibility: They must expect it and help provide the educational system to bring it about.

Recommendations

1. Develop strategic planning and programs with fund-raising aimed at soliciting endowments earmarked for sick and injured animals. For animal control organizations, funding is limited. It is very difficult for government agencies to develop systems to treat injured animals. If this problem is to be addressed, it must come from the nonprofits.

2. Develop programs that use donations to care for and rehabilitate sick and injured animals. The San Francisco SPCA has developed the *Cinderella Rehabilitation and Medical Treatment Fund*. More than 1.6 million dollars has been donated to help sick animals.
   Another successful program is the *Indigent Animal Medical Care Fund* operated in San Diego, Calif.. This program creates a fund whereby veterinarians administer to injured animals whose owners are unknown. They receive compensation for discounted services. Donation canisters are placed in clinics and hospitals to raise funds.

Factor Twelve

Programs to detect uneducated owners or owners that are experiencing problems and intervene with appropriate education

Situation

"There is no such thing as a bad dog, only uninformed owners."

A major study of relinquishment factors related to dogs and cats was conducted by the National Council on Pet Population (Salman et. el. 1998). Results from exit interviews with 3,772 former owners who relinquished their animals revealed only 4% of their dogs were enrolled in a dog training class, 1% had a private lesson and 1% sent their dog to a professional trainer. Most attempted training themselves (62.5%).[44]

Of the people who surrender their pet, (53% of the dog owners and 58% of cat owners) believe animals misbehave out of spite (contrary to well-established training knowledge). Additionally, 34% of dog owners and 29% of cat owners thought that rubbing the animal's nose in its mess would help to house train the pet. This is contrary to well-established training knowledge.

The most common behavioral conditions reported for cats were acting fearful, hyperactivity and house soiling. The most common behavioral conditions reported for dogs were hyperactivity, damage to house (usually chewing), house soiling and barking. Owners of 12% of dogs and 9% of cats reported the animal had bitten someone. The incidences of relinquished animals that had attacked other animals was insignificant.

The majority of people who pay for training classes are those who recognize the value and cost of education. They have sums of discretionary income. The average person is quick to say, "I can train the animal," but most of the time he/she hasn't a clue. When things go wrong, these owners are quick to blame the animal. Eventually, because of unresolved conditions that impede companionship, the relationship grows tedious and they get rid of the pet.

Recommendation

1. Establish a system to detect incompetent pet owners and provide the requisite training at an affordable cost. A testing system could be used similar to obtaining a driver's license. People who fail the exam would be required to take a FREE, one night, two-hour pet owner orientation session. This workshop would cover all the basic behaviors that people need to know to properly care for their pet. The class would provide informational handouts for future reference.

2. Require first-time owners to attend a pet-owner orientation seminar given by a highly respected, experienced animal behaviorist. These first-time owners cause major unwitting abuse.

3. Use pre-adoption counseling and align expectations with reality.

4. Offer books to people conducting a search for a dog or cat. A book like *Choosing and Caring for a Shelter Dog* is an excellent primer.

Factor Thirteen

Full support from the veterinary community

Situation

The veterinary profession has changed considerably since the 1950s. The primary role of veterinary medicine in the '50s was to help the agriculture industry supply wholesome and safe products by rearing better and healthier livestock. Today, with the shift in population from farms to urban areas, the number of small-animal doctors has grown to respond to the need for companion animal health care. Small animal practitioners, once considered nonessential by their large animal counterparts, now represent about 73% of practices.

Veterinarians have always been diligently concerned with an animal's physical health. They respond to injuries and treat diseases with knowledge and skill. Animals are living longer and are generally healthier through preventative medicine. Unfortunately, with the changing role of the veterinarian, there has not been a corresponding change in their resolve to stop the needless destruction of companion animals.

Although a veterinarian is regarded as a health-care practitioner, his/her primary responsibility goes much further. Animal owners look to veterinarians to heal, to save animal lives and to relieve animal suffering. More importantly, people look to veterinarians as their primary source for advice on the overall well-being of their pets. To answer the challenge of becoming a no-kill nation, veterinarians must work with clients to lower birth rates of companion animals through spay/neuter surgery and they must educate uninformed owners who provoke behavior problems.

Veterinarians are caught in a moral dilemma, the heart of which is money. They are business people and can't afford to lose money. Most practitioners incur large debts from schooling and start-up costs associated with their practice. They have families, mortgages and practices with bills to pay. Free or low-cost sterilization surgery is costly, and veterinarians should not be required to bear the brunt of those costs. Compared to other professions with similar educational requirements, their incomes are not high.

"Veterinarians are naturally committed to animal welfare! In my experience, concern for animals is the main reason people go into veterinary medicine. They are trained scientists. As a group, they are highly intelligent. Their work puts them in daily and dramatic contact with the tragic consequences of irresponsible pet ownership. If anyone can speak knowledgeably for the rights of pet animals, it is veterinarians."

— Bernard Rollin

Sterilization surgery is primarily responsible for reducing the amount of animals killed in shelters, from a high in the early seventies of 20% to today's rate of around 5%. If no intervention programs were utilized, it is estimated we would be killing 22 million animals, instead of the 6 million we currently euthanize.

Remarkably, 76% of veterinarians participated in low-cost sterilization programs, according to a national study conducted by *Animal People* for *Spay U.S.A.*. They did so because "They wanted to help the animals," and felt a "sense of professional duty." The majority used profits from regular-priced sterilizations to offset losses from the discounted program.

Most veterinarians complain that 1) clients appeared able to pay full price, 2) clients were not repeat customers. Pet owners complained 1) they couldn't find a vet with a program, 2) had to pay for unexpected services and 3) the cost (was) still too high.

Veterinarians' main concerns are that too many people are not paying full price and that programs are not being used by the truly needy. Conversely, studies show most people who obtain low-cost sterilization surgery wouldn't have their animals altered if a low-cost service was not available.[2]

Sterilization surgery is primarily responsible for reducing the number of animals killed in shelters. It has helped lower percentages from a high of 21% in the early 1970s to 5% in 1996. If no intervention programs were utilized, it is estimated we would be killing 22 million animals, instead of 6 million.

In addition, as victims of unknowing owners, more animals are displaced from homes for behavior reasons than are lost for health reasons. Veterinarians must be more than surgeons and diagnosticians. They must be leaders in making sure owners know how to properly socialize and train their puppies. Owners must be able to turn to veterinarians for problem solving.

Veterinarians have a social and moral obligation to help put an end to the surplus dog and cat tragedy. They must use their knowledge, influence and resources to reduce the number of animals going into shelters and help stop the killing of healthy companion animals.

Early Age Spay/Neuter

Early age altering refers to spays and neuters done between the ages of six and fourteen weeks. Waiting until they were over six months of age was recommended primarily as a precaution because of questionable anesthetic effects. In addition, veterinarians were concerned with increased incidences of lower urinary tract disease, skeletal development and effects on behavior.

Surgical sterilization remains the most effective means of population control. When this surgery is delayed, it increases the chance of accidental litters. It is estimated that 20% of breedings come from people who intended to have their pet sterilized, but the pet was impregnated before it had the surgery.[50]

A study, *Early Altering, Developmental and Behavioral Effect of Prepubertal Gonadectomy in the Domestic Cat*, by Mark S. Bloomberg, DVM, MS, Dip. ACVS; University of Florida has found the procedure safe and effective.

Recommendations

1. Join forces or start an area council to end needless killing.

2. Support spay/neuter and early age spay/neuter programs.

3. Educate clients. Education must be more aggressively undertaken by companion animal veterinarians. Animal welfare organizations only see a small portion of animal owners. The task of public education falls to veterinarians. In accepting this task, veterinarians could be a

tremendous force for positive change. *Sell* every owner on having his/her pet altered immediately instead of waiting until the animal is six months, as normally recommended. Explain to resistant clients, in no uncertain terms, that sterilization has health benefits, improves undesirable behaviors, eliminates estrus in females, lowers license fees and reduces veterinary expenses over the life of the animal. Procrastination leads to pregnancy.

4. People who bond with and enjoy their pets are likely to become more responsible and better-informed and keep their pets longer. They will depend on the veterinary-client relationship like new parents depends on a pediatrician. Better client retention means greater revenues.

5. Assist and support feral cat trapping programs (TVARM) and feral cat spay/neuters. Cats account for 60% of animals killed in shelters. The main problem with cats stems from feral and free-roamers. Trapped cats can be handled efficiently if the right cages are used.

6. Create a county-funded voucher program for altering of unowned cats.

7. Include behavior courses and certification in veterinary school curricula. Schools must include classes on the dynamics of pet overpopulation and the veterinarian's role in combating the problem, the human-animal bond, health implications, zoonotic information and owner education.

8. Develop veterinary school teaching programs or internships with community shelter clinics in exchange for scholarships and or endowments.

9. Conduct research on alternatives to surgical birth control.

10. Offer dog training classes and have a trained behaviorist on call at every clinic or hospital. Annual check-ups should include behavior as well as health.

11. "Sell" early age spay/neutering. Only 5% of pet kittens are acquired from shelters. Neutering of all kittens prior to adoption from a shelter can have only a minor effect on the cat overpopulation problem. On the other hand, if veterinarians in clinical practice were to recommend spay/neutering kittens at an early age to preclude any births, a major decrease in unwanted cats could result.

12. "Sell" identification programs. Join together with your local veterinary association and strongly recommend permanent ID.

13. Package low-cost sterilization with vaccinations and identifications at a nominal price. Veterinarians must schedule puppies around eight weeks of age to evaluate socialization (especially around children), temperament, biting inhibition and destructive behaviors. The visit should require 30 minutes. Veterinarians should require owners to view the video "Sirius Puppy Training" by Ian Dunbar and have these videos to loan.

Remarkably, 76% of veterinarians participated in low-cost sterilization programs according to a national study conducted by Animal People for Spay USA.

The Veterinarian's Role

from Animal Rights and Human Morality

by Bernard E. Rollin, Ph. D.

Dr. Rollin is professor of physiology and biophysics, director of Bioethical Studies at Colorado State University Veterinary School and a world-renown spokesperson on ethical animal issues. (Rev. ed. Prometheus Books 1992)

It is hard to imagine anyone more suited for active involvement in solving the pet problem than the veterinarian. In the first place, simple self-interest dictates that veterinarians, at least the pet animal veterinarians, ought to be concerned with a social situation that threatens the very basis of their livelihood. After all, there is always the danger, as has happened in parts of Europe, that pet animals will be banned altogether, especially in urban areas. It would really take only one zoonotic epidemic, traceable to the dog, in a place like New York City where the feelings about dog feces already run high, for a strong anti-pet reaction. If pets were banned or if the conditions for keeping pets became too restrictive, the veterinarian would be out of a job. For this reason alone, it would behoove the veterinarian to take the initiative in solving the pet problem.

But the reasons for veterinarians' participating in dealing with this issue run far deeper. The essential *raison d'etre* for the veterinarian is the health and welfare of animals. I often pose two models to my veterinary students and to the audiences of veterinarians whom I address and ask them which model is closest to their ideal of their profession. One model compares the veterinarian to an auto mechanic, and the animal to a car. Consider a car owner who brings an automobile into a garage. The mechanic informs him that it will cost X number of dollars to fix the car. The car owner decides it is not worth it, tells the mechanic to junk the car, and the mechanic shrugs. On this view, a veterinarian ought to be simply the agent or tool of the owner, a simple extension of the owner's concern or lack of it. This is, of course, the model that society and the law forces upon the veterinarian: the property model. But we are concerned with what ought to be, and most veterinarians find it abhorrent to destroy or not treat an animal that

can be restored to health, simply because the owner doesn't wish to spend the money. On the other model, the veterinarian is like a pediatrician. Though the parents pay the bills, they cannot tell the pediatrician not to cure the child because they don't wish to spend the money or don't have it. (It is their acceptance of this model that leads many veterinarians to do a good deal of unpaid work.)

This, incidentally, illustrates a possible impact of animal rights as far as veterinary medicine is concerned. On the view we have expounded, an animal ought not simply be a piece of property, and no animal should be denied life and health because of the owner's whim or unwillingness to pay. On the other hand, the veterinarian should not be forced to bear the financial burden either.

Veterinarians are (or ought to be) more knowledgeable concerning animal welfare, physical and psychological, than any other group of citizens. Thus they ought to be pioneering in developing rational legislation aimed at solving the pet problem and, even more importantly, they ought to be educating their clients and the general public regarding animals and responsible pet ownership. (Such educational efforts, if conducted in public forums such as lectures or courses offered through the humane societies, could also provide invaluable public exposure and advertisement for the veterinarian, which in turn would be likely to result in a much enhanced practice.) Given these moral and pragmatic reasons for veterinarian involvement in the pet problem, why has there in fact been, relatively speaking, so little of it? And why, when there has been veterinarian involvement, has it tended to come only as a reaction to some truly oppressive idiotic ordinance or policy that directly threatens their earning capacity?

There are many reasons for this. In the first place, the animal welfare movement has often tended to see low-cost spay and neuter clinics as the major step in solving the pet problem, and veterinarians are concerned about the effects of such clinics on their income - an income that, on the average, is not very high. But this does not seem to be the major reason, for veterinarians have learned to live with and sometimes even support these clinics. The deeper reasons for lack of massive veterinarian involvement in animal welfare work must be sought elsewhere.

Perhaps the most important reason can be traced to issues pertaining to veterinary and human medical education, and to science education in general. The main thrust of this education seems to be the mastery of techniques and facts. Until very recently, virtually no emphasis has been placed in veterinary curricula on the moral and social dimensions of veterinary medicine. The educational process is far too reductionistic and mechanistic. The practice of veterinary medicine is taught as if it were value-neutral, and it is assumed that students will simply pick up the moral and social implications of what they do when they are in practice. Unfortunately, this very often doesn't happen, any more than physicians pick up expertise in evaluating moral and social problems in human medicine. What, in fact, happens is that these problems are ignored.

Yet in point of fact, these problems are central to the practice of veterinary medicine, as more and more practitioners and educators are realizing. They are important not only for economic reasons, but also for medical reasons. All medicine is played out in the social arena.

A veterinarian cannot merely be technically competent. Even to be a good diagnostician, he or she must be able to communicate on a variety of levels and must understand that the symptoms being described by the owner are being filtered through personal and cultural biases. Technical competence is only a necessary condition for being a good veterinarian. Veterinarians must realize that many malpractice suits arise out of failure on the part of a veterinarian to communicate with a client, not out of incompetence.

A major part of the social problems with pet animals stems from ignorance of the animals nature or "telos." Veterinarians are usually good sources of information concerning the physical anatomy, requirements, interests and needs of the animal. Yet when it comes to the mind of the animal, the psychological and behavioral aspects of the animals' telos, the veterinarian too often is lacking. It is very unlikely that the veterinarian has had a single course in animal behavior, behavioral pathology or training, yet the lives of pet animals often depend upon the veterinarian's ability to successfully resolve problems like a pet who

housesoils, a pet that destroys furniture or a pet who roams.

In short it appears that veterinarians have not taken a more active role in dealing with the enormously complex cluster of issues involved in the "pet problem," primarily because they are not trained to worry about these questions. Organized veterinary medicine must also share the blame. Outside of occasional letters to the editor (for many years by or against Michael Fox), veterinary journals have published very little on the moral and social dimensions of veterinary medicine, although this is beginning to change.

For a long time, for example, to most practitioners veterinary medical ethics (like human medical ethics to physicians) meant the sort of issues dealt with in the American Veterinary Medical Association's code of ethics, which is really a code of professional etiquette dealing with such issues as advertising, disseminating medical information to the public and maintaining a 4 6 professional" image. Happily, things are beginning to change. Conferences are being held on the social and moral aspects of veterinary medicine and articles are appearing in the AVMA Journal. (The Journal devoted an entire issue to the pet overpopulation problem.) Veterinary colleges are beginning to develop courses on animal behavior. And the pressure brought on by public concern with all aspects of the pet problem - be it methods of euthanasia or attempts to limit the number of dogs a person can own, is certain to further stimulate veterinarians to involve themselves with these issues.

This is all to the good. Veterinarians are naturally committed to animal welfare and concern for animals is the main reason people go into veterinary medicine. Veterinarians are trained scientists. As a group, they are highly intelligent. Their work puts them in daily and dramatic contact with the tragic consequences of irresponsible pet ownership. If anyone can speak knowledgeably for the rights of pet animals, it is the veterinarian. Most important, their work provides them with a natural forum for educating a significant portion of the pet-owning public.

Let us hope that we can anticipate and work toward the time when animal advocates and veterinarians have forged a solid bond of cooperation and work effectively together as spokespersons for the moral and legal rights of animals.

Factor Fourteen
Educational programs that define the problem, prioritize resources and initiate solutions that change owner behaviors

Situation

There is only one real solution. We must take aggressive action to educate the public to the enormity of the surplus pet problem and instill a commitment by every animal person to a goal of *zero pet population growth.* We must become a no-kill nation! The public must be made to feel, as well as to understand, the need for a change in the status quo. The task is formidable because results demand not only a change of heart but a change in people's behavior.

For many people, concern about pet overpopulation focuses primary on the rates of killing associated with various shelters. Pet overpopulation is then seen as the individual shelter's problem (if not fault) when, in reality, the shelter is dealing with the whole community's disposal of its pets. Changing this perception involves convincing pet owners of their participation in the cause of the problem and of the importance of their participation in the solutions.

Many pet owners view the problem in conceptual terms. They don't consider the consequences of their casual indifference to sterilization. They don't realize that they subject a portion of their accidental litter to death. They mean well. They try frantically to place the pets, but only have luck with a few. No one wants the rest, so they take them to the shelter. One animal or "just one litter" from one person, does not seem like an insurmountable problem. What they don't realize is 10, 20 or 50 people are bringing animals into an already crowded shelter every day. Space is precious. As a result, animals die. [30]

A definite change of conscience has occurred since the 1960s. Thirty years ago, breeding a dog or cat was taken to be a good and natural thing. People saw nothing wrong with producing one more litter. People knew very little about spay/neuter and were callously indifferent about birth control for pets. From that view, we've passed to one in which most people regard boundless animal reproduction as a bad thing. Now, we must reach those who remain indifferent and let them know they are part of the problem. Getting people to make this change of heart and conscience is one of our greatest challenges.

Animal welfare groups have been the traditional champions of sterilization over the past 30 years. They have been ambitious in their efforts to promote the message of spay/neuter. Brochures, special events, fliers, ads, public-service messages, low-cost spay/neutering vouchers and clinics have resulted in as many as 81% of metropolitan community animals being sterilized, a wonderful accomplishment since the dark years of the 70s.

Sterilization alone will not solve the problem of pet abuse. Although one can develop methods to spay and neuter multitudes of animals in simple and ingenious ways, this will not stop people from euthanizing animals for trivial reasons or failing to understand and provide for an animals' needs. These problems can be attacked only by changing the way people think. [41]

An educational revolution must be instigated by people for whom the issue is of paramount concern. Sheltering agencies are the leading proponents of humane education; they serve as the public's primary association with this issue. However, only a small percentage of animals are acquired from shelters. For an educational strategy to be effective it must be implemented on a grass roots level by an alliance of organizations and individuals; by veterinary practices, dog trainers, groomers, pet-supply stores and, most importantly, peer pressure.

Animal rights advocates, in their zeal to end the problem, have presented a morbid image to the general public. The traditional approach has been to appeal to people's emotions by chronicling atrocities through appalling visual images, like showing an animal being injected with sodium pentobarbital or showing barrels of dead animals. Unfortunately, although compelling to some, this display of death turns most people off. They avoid becoming activists or even going to a shelter to adopt an animal because it is just too depressing to see the animals on ''death row.''

Emotion is essential for moral action. However, it must be tempered with reason. There are few, if any, advertising campaigns that use negative emotion to sell a product. Most campaigns emphasize the life-enhancing qualities and features of the product. Rational arguments are more effective when they include owner responsibility, animal care and the wonders of pets as companions, playmates and friends. There are millions of testimonials.

There is much to be done in public education. The animal movement has done a good job in using the national media to argue its case, however, little is done to modify behaviors of pet-owning households.

Humane societies and SPCAs must question whether they are doing all they can to impart to the public the urgency and importance of the pet overpopulation crisis. Generally, a small portion of the budget goes to educational outreach about pet overpopulation (usually school programs), but the bulk of money goes to the direct care of animals. Are animal protectors doing all they can to advance public education and change behaviors?

Traditional humane education has focused on two main areas: classroom education for children and spay/neuter programs. Two significant factors that lead to euthanasia are failure by owners to solve common behavior problems and the proliferation by unaltered and free-roaming feral cats. It is imperative to recognize the need for pet owner training and elevate its importance in our educational mission to protect animals. Equal in the mandate is an educational program which strongly urges people who feed or ''loosely own'' feral cats to spay/neuter those animals.

The bulk of activity for many organizations consists of staff humane educators visiting schools to impart lessons of humane animal care. Although helpful, animal welfare groups must question whether this approach is on target to end the needless killing of animals in shelters. Because funding is always limited, this activity would be better served by developing volunteers to visit schools, perhaps people who have teaching backgrounds.

The problem of pet abuse will not be solved through sterilization alone. Although one can develop methods to spay and neuter multitudes of animals in simple and ingenious ways, this will not stop people from euthanizing animals for trivial reasons or failing to understand and provide for an animals' needs. These problems can be attacked only by changing the way people think.
Bernard Rollin Ph. D.

It is imperative to recognize the need for pet owner training and elevate its importance in our educational mission to protect animals. Equally important is a communications campaign to raise awareness for identification and educational programs which strongly urges people who feed or "loosely own" feral cats to spay/neuter those cats.

Recommendations

1. Expand the scope of humane education. Does everyone in your community know and understand the dynamics of pet overpopulation? Is there total focus on a unified information campaign by major factions of the pet community, such as veterinarians, all nonprofit shelter agencies, breeders, groomers, rescue groups, dog trainers and animal control authorities? Do individuals know what they can do to end the problem?

2. Those who care about animals must spearhead the effort to end this terrible tragedy. The most effective way to get the message across on pet overpopulation is for various animal organizations to join together in one combined community effort. Above and beyond the immediate gains, coalitions provide wonderful opportunities for sharing and developing ideas among the participating agencies and individuals. Coalitions present a unified message and utilize and coordinate available resources.

3. Reach new pet owners who do not initially seek veterinary care, dog training or shelter services. Community-intervention programs are needed to identify those owners and bring them into a network of training and preventive animal care. This highly challenging effort is ideally suited to a cooperative program involving animal welfare groups, dog clubs, and veterinarians.

4. Everyone should understand the urgency of action. Priorities must be set for the best use of staff and resources. Remember, public relation and humane education go hand-and-hand. We need to work smarter and use limited resources where they can effect the most change.

5. Focus resources on cats and on general public education (including the veterinary profession) about the existence of a serious feral cat overpopulation problem and about the importance of neutering cats before puberty. If people feed feral cats, they must understand the importance of trapping, spaying/neutering, and releasing.

6. To educate the community at large about the importance of spaying and neutering, messages must be repeated over and over again through a constant barrage of communication. Numerous public-service announcements, press releases, speeches, workshops. radio talk show visits, newspaper columns, stickers and decals can be used. Local publications are often happy to fill extra space with messages about spaying and neutering. Free publicity can be utilized with billboards and transit ads.

    Posters, fliers and brochures should be developed as a means to advertise the campaign. Communications should itemize the benefits of spay/neuter and should be distributed to breed clubs and breeders, groomers, pet stores and most importantly, veterinarian clinics. Veterinary practices need to be on the front line in educating the public on the importance of neutering their pet. They should be "selling it" to all owners.

Successful promotional campaigns are multipronged approaches which focus on the benefits of altering the pet rather than on the problem of pet overpopulation. They focus on cost savings, health benefits, preventing unwanted litters, improved behavior of neutered animals or preventing indoor spraying and marking of cats. Some innovative agencies use special event centered around "Spay Day."

Other methods used are to offer free surgeries to the first 100 people who call; volunteers handing out brochures at supermarkets; offers to neuter all male cats belonging to area residents free of charge during one 30-day period and offers of free surgery for unowned neighborhood cats before kitten season. They should use available educational videos that show the ease and safety of the neutering procedure.

7. Convince teachers that instilling an awareness of humane animal care is in the forefront of their responsibilities. In the long run, educating children is always important. With their natural love of animals, it's easy for children to see why animals should be spayed and neutered, and what they learn they pass on to family and friends.[9]

Teaching teachers how to integrate humane education into their classrooms should be a major objective for all community animal protection groups. Teacher curriculum guides should be promoted and used by schools, without exception. Curricula and lesson plans are readily available from leading organizations. Colleges and universities should also provide classes on the moral status of animals and human-animal interactions. Shelters should encourage class day trips; they present an ideal occasion to illustrate the consequences of social irresponsibility.

8. Design adult and community education programs. If we value an animal's life we must put in place a system of education that requires training for those found deficient in animal care skills. Tests should be given to determine capability. If lacking, new owners should be required to attend a class.

9. Put in place a system for providing the needed education relevant to caring for animals and solving problems. Studies revealed temperament and behavioral problems are responsible for the death of more dogs in shelters than are all the infectious diseases combined.

Many factors may influence whether a companion animal thrives or fails in a home. When a relationship between a person and an animal does not develop, the pet is often removed from the home.

Strategies should be focused on the education of new owners and their dogs. New owner orientation sessions, puppy and good manners classes, crisis intervention, advice to prospective new pet owners on acquiring a dog and animal behavior problem solving should be instituted in all communities and shelters should become the hub for all training activity. The same priority given to spay/neuter or disease vaccination programs should be given to training programs.

Humane societies and SPCAs must question whether they are doing all they can to impart to the public the urgency and importance of the pet overpopulation crisis. Generally, a small portion of a budget goes to educational outreach about pet overpopulation (usually school programs), but the bulk of money goes to the direct care of animals. Are animal protectors doing all they can to advance public education and change behaviors?

Thousands of trappers will be needed to humanely address the feral cat problem. They all need to be recruited and trained in responsible methods. They need to report on colony activities, use proper equipment, follow safe trapping procedures and have a procedure for working with veterinarians.

10. Veterinary preventive-care programs should include increased contact with clients during the pet's first three months of ownership, a time when most problems occur. Prevention programs should also include close contact with dog owners during the fragile juvenile and young adult years — the period which has the greatest risk of relinquishment. A temperament test should be administered with strong recommendations for training, if needed.

11. Recruit and train hundreds of feral cat trappers to humanely address the feral problem. They all need to be trained in responsible methods, report on colony activities, use proper equipment, follow safe trapping procedures and have a procedure for working with veterinarians.

12. Obtain more funding for scientific research relating to companion animal welfare.

13. Return stray dogs home. One significant way to reduce the population of pets in shelters is to return identifiable animals home. Stray dogs make up a large portion of dogs killed in shelters. Traditionally, animal welfare organizations rely on license sales to return lost dogs home. Unfortunately, the majority of people do not license their dogs. In California, records from 1996 revealed approximately 2 million licensed dogs out of an estimated population of 6 million. This seems to be the norm.

Animal control organizations should strongly consider using the owner's telephone number as the license number. They may lose impoundment income, but fewer dogs will be admitted to shelters, which means less strain on capacity and less killing. Educational efforts should include bus billboards advertising, license applications in veterinarians' waiting rooms and efforts to increase rabies and license data bases.

License sales have also been increased by 1) publishing applications in local newspapers, 2) publishing names of delinquent dog owners in newspapers, 3) recruiting volunteers to conduct door-to-door canvassing, 4) offering a "bounty" for licenses sold, 5) canvassing neighborhoods to identify homes where pets are kept, with a follow-up visits at addresses where no current pet license is on record, 6) increasing the availability of license application forms by mail distribution, 7) offering special low-cost or free rabies vaccination clinics where the license tag is included or required and 8) advertising "significant" fines for harboring an unlicensed pet.

Individual Responsibilities

1. Spay/neuter your pet at an early age, well before sexual maturity (by four months). Encourage your friends and others to do the same.

2. Don't be an uneducated owner. Most pet owners experience problems. Have the knowledge and confidence to work out any problem. Take a basic dog obedience class. Learn about basic dog and cat behavior. The internet is an abundant source of information.

3. Safeguard your pet. Don't let your pet roam.

4. Make sure identification is in place and secured. Use a microchip and visual identification tags.

5. Adopt a pet from an animal shelter, purebred or all breed rescue or reputable purebred breeder. Don't use the local classifieds.

6. If you have the slightest inclination to breed your pet and have never done so, don't. Leave breeding to knowledgeable, experienced professionals dedicated to improving the health and temperament of the breed, have quality breeding stock, guarantee their animals and have established an excellent reputation. These individuals assume responsibility for the pet throughout its lifetime. If you have to relinquish the pet, they will take it back and adopt it to another good home.

   "Just One Litter" contributes to the pet overpopulation crisis. Too many stray and unwanted pets are the product of amateur or accidental breeding. When a pet is born from amateur breeding, chances are it will be condemned to a life of misery, deprivation and death.

7. Make responsible donations. Support your local nonprofit humane society, shelter and low-cost spay/neuter organization with financial donations or by volunteering your services.

8. Take responsibility for your pet. If, for whatever reason, you need to give up your pet, make every effort to seek a solution to the problem. Check with your friends and neighbors. Don't kid yourself into thinking someone will come to the shelter and give your dog a home on his/her farm. Statistics tell us that approximately 60% of all dogs and 80% of all cats that enter shelters will be euthanized. If your pet is over the age of two, it will have a slim chance of being adopted. Don't place an ad that says, "Free to good home." Many of those dogs end up in research labs, in the hands of brokers or someone who is not committed to the responsibilities of pet ownership. Chances are it will soon end up at a shelter.

9. If your pet is experiencing behavior problems, seek the help of a trained professional. Call your veterinarian or pet store and ask for a referral to a good behaviorist or trainer. Many problems are unknowingly caused by owner-handling errors.

10. If you are going to move, take your pet with you. Talk to your future landlord and explain that you have a well-behaved pet. Take and pass a basic obedience class or AKC Good Citizenship Test and show the certificate to your landlord. Offer to make a pet-security deposit that will protect the owner from financial loss to his or her property. Don't sign a lease until you know the property accepts pets.

11. Be a good neighbor. Don't allow excessive barking, soiling or free roaming.

Don't be part of the problem. Be part of the solution!

The problem is that human interests are protected by rights in general and by the right to own property in particular. As far as the law is concerned, an animal is the personal property, or chattel, of the animal's owner and cannot possess rights. Indeed, it is a fundamental premise of our property law that property cannot itself have rights as against human owners and that, as property, animals are objects of the exercise of human property rights.

— Gary L. Francione, co-founder of the Rutgers Animal Rights Law Center

Factor Fifteen
Animal legislation on which all organizations can agree

Situation

A high concentration of animals coming into close relationship with people causes problems. Citizens demand that public officials control people who carelessly disregard their responsibilities as good neighbors. They require government to protect them from the dangers of bites and disease caused by free-roaming animals. The public expects the government to enact and enforce laws to contend with animal problems.

Animals are considered property in most jurisdictions, without legal standing. This means law enforcement officials can take action without depriving their owners of their constitutional rights. It also means that cruelty laws cannot be passed on their behalf. Successful cruelty laws are enacted because abuse offends human sensibilities.

The status of animals will not change until we legally recognize the intrinsic value of companion animals. To date, no court has extended legal rights to animals.

Laws typically feature regulations that address the collection of stray and unwanted animals, licensing and rabies vaccination of dogs, regulation of animal behavior, health permits for dog kennels, bites, quarantine, cruelty, keeping animals on premises and the impoundment of animals.

Although we have laws to protect the public from animals, we have no laws to protect animals from being killed by society. Despite the enormous surplus of cats and dogs in shelters and their subsequent killing, there has been little scientific data defining the source of the problem. Only a handful of communities have commissioned studies to determine the pet population dynamics in their region. Consequently, coercive laws are passed that are not based on facts, but assumptions.

A common view in the animal rights community says there are too many animals and therefore breeders are the culprits. They are over-proliferating the nation with a constant supply of cats and dogs. Closer examination of the facts show breeders play a very small role in the matrix.

Of people that relinquish dogs, the root problem can be traced to a failure to properly train a dog and solve ordinary behavior problems and a lack of commitment by owners. Newborn puppies account for less than 1% of shelter admits. Animals are in homes and coming out of homes. Overpopulation for dogs is minimal.

Pedigree cats account for only 3% of the total cat population. Surveys have found these cats to be under represented in shelters, with a very small number killed. Purebred cat breeders are not the problem.

Breeders have been unfairly targeted by animal rights activists and the Humane Society of the United States. HSUS has employed breeder bans, moratoriums and legislative initiatives in an attempt to prohibit breeding.

In December 1990, California's San Mateo County passed the nation's first law that attempted to end pet overpopulation by enacting legislation requiring dog and cat owners to buy a breeding license or get their pets sterilized. The ordinance initially called for a 6-month moratorium on the breeding of all dogs and cats. If, at the end of that time, the pet population did not reach "zero growth," anyone without a breeding license would be prohibited from owning an adult dog or cat that has not been spayed or neutered and violators would face fines of up to $500.

The ordinance was initiated by the Peninsula Humane Society, the only animal shelter in the county. The San Mateo County Board of Supervisors received more public comment on the breeding ban than on any other issue the board had addressed.

San Mateo Entry/Exit Numbers			
Admit	**Reclaimed**	**Adopted**	**Euthanized**
1990 4986	2677	1739	1281
1991 6694	2232	1385	1200
1992 4332	2175	1445	1355
1993 5121	2419	1427	1269
1994 4355	2082	1268	1001
1995 4893	2399	1287	1250
1996 4922	2462	1186	1266

According to statistics from the California Department of Health, in 1990, the year before the breeder ordinance, San Mateo county impounded 4,986 dogs and euthanized 1281. In 1991, the year after the bill was passed, the county impounded 6,694 (a 34% increase), with a reported 1200 euthanized. (This euthanasia number is highly suspicious. If, of the 6,694 dogs impounded, 2,232 were reclaimed and 1,385 were adopted, there are 1,877 dogs unaccounted for as exiting the shelter. If these dogs were euthanized, total euthanisias would exceed 3,000, more than double the average rate.) Obviously, the only impact the bill had on the community was to increase impoundment and perhaps euthanasias.

The Atlanta Humane Society, which also performs animal control for Fulton County, Ga., embarked on a campaign to strengthen ordinances with an effort to educate judges and prosecutors about community problems attributable to pet overpopulation. Atlanta instituted specific days and courts for animal cases. First offenders for "dog-at-large" routinely received fines of $200, suspended on proof of fence or run construction. With increased penalties, the Atlanta Humane Society experienced a sharp increase in the number of dogs handled as people relinquished rather than pay fines or construct an area for confinement.

A California woman who rescues cats kept ten to fifteen cats in her home, fed them and provided medical care at her own expense, advertising to find good homes. Her neighbor complained. Animal control responded, cited her for a violation of local limit laws. The cats were confiscated, brought to the shelter. Due to lack of space, the cats were killed. There was nothing anyone could do. The animal control officer did his job and followed the law. Because the situation was complaint driven, the law, not reason, prevailed. Laws made to protect people can have dire consequences for animals.

Caring and commitment can't be mandated. Unfounded, coercive legislation only serves to alienate responsible individuals and prevent the unity that is needed from concerned people and organizations.

The first law that is needed is a law that requires all shelters to provide accurate entry and exit statistics (separating dogs and cats) to a state reporting agency.

A 1997 Northwestern University study by Arluke and Luke found that 401 cases, only 15% of the alleged animal abuse cases got into courts, with 8% of abusers drawing jail time.

Strays account for close to 75% of dogs that enter California animal control shelters. Most areas have laws that require dogs to be licensed. Despite these laws, dogs go unlicensed and untagged. Courts are crammed and enforcement officers are too busy with higher priorities. It's costly to produce promotional campaigns to encourage compliance. As a result, we have an ineffective identification program to which we are firmly committed.

Sadly, legislation to prevent the abuse of animals is another area for disappointment. A 1997 Northwestern University study by Arluke and Luke found that in 401 cases, only 15% of the alleged animal abuse cases got into courts, with 8% of abusers drawing jail time.

We have laws that require dogs to be on a leash and licensed, but over 50% of dogs in shelters are strays. We have laws against urinating and defecation, yet we still have to tiptoe through city sidewalks. Just as society's behavior was changed regarding heart disease, public behavior must be modified in animal care and responsibility through educational means. People who count on legislation to solve the problem of surplus and unwanted animals will be disappointed. Judges, prosecutors and law enforcement officials do not deem animals a meaningful priority.

In general, laws don't protect animals, they protect people. They give people the legal authority to destroy animals. In Colorado, a dog can be shot if he wanders in the area of livestock, cats can be killed if they have attacked a bird and police can shoot any dog they deem "vicious." (Is barking vicious?)

Cat Licensing

All cats deserve loving, permanent homes with responsible care givers that safely confine and care for their cat's needs. This is the goal of all animal protectors. However, millions of cats do not fit this category and are at risk from current legislative efforts to license cats.

Many communities are turning to cat legislation as a panacea that will solve the problems of surplus cats. According to proponents, mandatory cat licensing will put an end to the problem of stray and abandoned cats, raise the status of felines, increase funding for budget-strapped animal control agencies and make cat owners more responsible. All we need to do is pass a law. It sounds too good to be true. In reality, it is.

Major components for laws require all cats to be licensed, confined or supervised when outdoors; have identification, vaccination and sterilization; and mandate all care givers (including feral colony caretakers) to register with animal control. A registration fee is also required by all care givers. "People will be compelled to do the right thing simply because it's the law," according to *Animal Sheltering*, a publication of the Humane Society of the United States.

As is the case with most animal-related legislation, (because animals have no legal status in America) laws are passed not to protect animals, but to benefit people. For cats, the stakes are high. In this case, millions of cats, found to be in violation of the law, could lose their lives. Cats that are loved, precious members of American households are in danger of being inadvertently swept up and killed, simply because they are unidentified.

Cat caretakers are also at risk of financial penalties. These caretakers will have to pay license fees, a "cat tax" on each cat they care for or face citations, fines, penalties, and possible confiscation of the animals they love. Thousands of caretakers make sure a shy and reclusive neighborhood cat has daily sustenance. At their personal expense, caretakers work tirelessly to feed, foster and rehabilitate feral cats and kittens and maintain feral colonies. Licensing laws will hamper efforts and force many compassionate caretakers, many with limited means, to stop providing for homeless cats. More cats will be left to fend for themselves, with fewer people to help them.

Many people casually or loosely own cats. These compassionate people provide abandoned, free-roaming cats with food, love and shelter in or around their homes. Unfortunately, their commitment to these cats is fragile. If money becomes a factor, many people will simply forfeit the cat. They will deny owning the cat explaining they were just providing food. Irresponsible owners won't be affected. They will ignore the law, cat licensing would be no exception. If cat licensing is enforced, they are likely to surrender or abandon their animals, which will only add to the number of cats killed.

Failure to comply with the law means impoundment into shelters where only two cats (mostly kittens) in ten come out alive. Adult feral cats are unadoptable. They will die as soon as their mandatory hold expires. Additionally, a great deal of animal control work involves responding to citizen complaints. License laws give angry, cat-hating neighbors more authority to order the seizure of a neighbor's roaming cat — a loved and cherished pet occasionally allowed outdoors for exercise.

The simple fact is licensing laws explicitly authorize the impoundment and killing of millions of cats, just for being unlicensed. A good portion of these impounded cats will be a cherished family member, rounded-up by unwitting animal control officers and by spiteful neighbors.

What's very disturbing is the fact that these laws are being passed with very little objective scientific study, free of political agendas. If studies were referenced, they would discover these critical facts:

- No one uniform entity can be defined as "the indigenous cat." There is a continuum of lifestyles between the feral cat existence and that of the pampered household pet. To understand the nature of cats is to recognize the great diversity that exists within the species. Some are truly domesticated, part of people's homes and lives, while others survive in the wild, avoiding humans and become part of the ecosystem It is important to acknowledge the different segments of the cat population, understanding the relationship between humans and recognize the cats ecological role.

- Almost every neighborhood in America has feral unsocialized cats that subsist in self-regulating colonies of similar cats living primarily on human refuse and vermin.

- Because cats exhibit varying degrees of sociability, even an animal care and control professional may not immediately be able to identify the difference between a feral cat and a frightened owned cat that is out roaming the neighborhood without identification.

Strays account for close to 75% of animals that enter California animal control shelters. Most areas have laws that require dogs to be licensed. Despite the presence of laws, dogs go unlicensed and untagged. Courts are crammed. Enforcement officers are too busy with higher priorities. It's costly to produce promotional campaigns to encourage compliance. As a result, animals die despite the presence of laws.

- Many owners fail to put collars with identification on their cat, fearing the cat will strangle. Many owners who try to obey the law and use break-away collars lose the tags when the collar does as it is intended.

- Unowned, feral and free-roaming cats comprise 40% more cats than owned cats, roughly 40 to 60 million in America.

- Close to two-thirds of the public allow its cats to roam outdoors. These owners are committed to the idea this it is necessary for the pet's well-being and happiness. Many of these owners are good, law abiding citizens. When owners are confronted with mandates that contradict their perception of a cat's needs, they discreetly resist those mandates.

- Over 80% of owned, household cats are sterilized. The vast majority of feral cats are not.

- Attempts to eradicate feral free-roaming cats by trapping and killing have not proven successful. Due to the presence of a consistent food source, new colonies quickly emerge.

- Fertile feral and free-roaming cats supply over two-thirds of the kittens to American households and supply the major source of surplus cats.

Cat licensing will not result in more cats returned to owners. King County, WA has had cat licensing for more than 25 years. Last year, 165 cats were returned to owners in King County, about 2% of all cats impounded and the national average.

Proposals to set a license fees at $15.00 would only slightly increase revenues after administrative and promotion expenses are deducted. Low compliance rates are historical.

If cat licensing is fully implemented and enforced it will result in more cats being impounded in shelters. The cats that have identification, are impounded and returned to owners will not offset increases in cats that are impounded, not claimed and consequently, euthanized. Cat legislation results in campaigns targeting unowned, feral and free roaming animals. Mandatory cat licensing will inadvertently kill many beloved household cats, increase the killing of unowned feral cats and have little effect on the surplus cat problem.

The Spirit of the Law

Caring and commitment can't be mandated. Unfounded, coercive legislation only serves to alienate responsible individuals and prevent the unity that is needed from concerned people and organizations.

Nothing is more harrowing to most animal lovers than to have animal control officers arrive on their property and confiscate their beloved pets. For people with limited incomes, fines and fees usually mean the pet will be forsaken. The goal of animal welfare groups should not be more restrictive laws but better care and responsibility — make better animal homes, not reduce the number of animal homes. A drastic decrease in the percentage of households that own dogs occurred from 1991 to 1996.

Responsible animal ownership will more likely come through the public moral conscience than law. Most people, Plato said, "Do not do evil knowingly." Most people want to have a best friend or companion; they just don't know how to achieve it.

Nationwide, statistical trends indicate major reductions in euthanasia through education and the public's willingness to do the right thing. Political agendas should not be advanced that are based on overblown euthanasia statistics used to create radical ordinances and restrictive regulations.

The enactment of any law makes us all less free.

Recommendations

1. Ensure proper funding for government-run animal control programs.

2. Governments should underwrite birth-rate reduction programs. Politicians and the public should be educated and know these programs are the most cost-efficient approach to the problem.

3. Test owners. If we deem the life of a pet valuable, we should appraise the fitness of the owner. An owner should be required to pass a test before acquiring a license to keep a pet. Every state requires testing to determine competence in areas they deem important. Test are taken for such activities as driving a car; obtaining a boating permit or in some states, a hunting permit. What is needed is testing or training to ensure that new owners are committed and qualified to be guardians who can responsibly care for a pet.

4. Require microchipping. Close to 78% of dogs that enter California animal control shelters have no identification. Kill rates could be cut in half if permanent identification was used.

5. Feature license numbers that use the owner's telephone number to prevent dogs from entering shelters, which overstresses their capacity. Shelters must bite the bullet and forgo impound fees in favor of lower kill rates. All animal groups should unite on this issue and seek a 100% compliance rate on licenses.

6. Animals are considered property. If your neighbor poisoned your beloved animal and your neighbor was found guilty, he would be liable for only the replacement cost of the animal in most states. There are current initiatives to declare the pet has sentimental value, much like an heirloom, thus deeming animals more valuable.

7. Institute differential licensing fees favoring spay/neutered animals.

8. Pass legislation that requires all sheltering agencies to provide accurate entry, exit and spay/neuter data to a central state agency. Data can then be collected on a national basis.

Nonprofits, including animal shelters, have been created to fill the need when government systems fail. Humane Societies and SPCAs are no different. They came into being as a result of limitations in government run animal control shelters. The nonprofit Humane Societies and SPCAs were a distinct alternative to the space and time limitations which resulted in an inordinate amount of killings at government run shelters. Unfortunately that distinct nonprofit mission is being slowly blurred as more shelters seek the financial security of animal control contracts.

Factor Sixteen
Increase the supply of rental apartments and condominium housing where pets are allowed

Situation
Animal organizations should work together to provide a solution to the dwindling supply of rental housing that accepts owners with animals. The main problem stems from property owners who lose money caused by damages. When amount of damage is not covered by deposits, owners suffer a loss and declare "no more pets." Irresponsible owners should be held accountable for damages above and beyond deposits, similar to rental-car agreements. Innovative programs provide landlords with bonds against pet damages. When property owners know they can't lose money, they will not discriminate against pet owners.

Recommendation

1. Develop a program that provides insurance against any loss in excess of pet deposits. Require an imprint from a major credit card similar to rental car companies. The law should be changed to allow landlords to charge credit cards for proven excessive damages caused by pets. This would open up more rentals if owners knew they would not suffer a loss.

2. Develop a free referral system to landlords who accept pets.

3. Make presentations to real estate associations and property managers.

Factor Seventeen
Better program accountability

Situation
What happens to animals when organizations don't fulfill their fiduciary responsibilities? Where is the check-and-balance system that keeps organizations striving for excellence for the animals? Are complaints to the mayor's office the only standard measurement of successful animal control programs?

Case Study — Midwest County Entry and Exit Statistics							
	Humane Soc.	%	Anml Cntl	%	Total	%	Nat Avg
Dog Admits	3,237		3,647		6,884	7.4	
Adopted	715	22	208	5.7	923	13.4	25
Returned to Owner	316	9.7	819	22.4	1,135	16.5	14
Euthanized	2,206	68.1	2,620	71.8	4,826	70.1	61
Cat Admits	5,219		1,815		7034	7.2	
Adopted	575	11.0	97	5.3	672	9.6	20
Returned to Owner	33	0.7	34	1.9	67	0.9	2
Euthanized	4,611	88.3	1,684	92.8	6295	89.5	78

County owned dog population = 92,186
Co Owned Cat Population = 97,911 (AVMA pet population survey)
Received 7.4% of total Co dog population
Received 7.2% of total Co owned cat population

One study of a nonprofit humane society and animal control service in a Midwest county illustrates the need for evaluation methods to help correct inefficiencies and halt unnecessary euthanasias. This county, with a population of just over 500,000 in 181,740 households, has a dog population of 92,756 with just 33,862 licenses issued. Each year there is a demand in the county for 11,130 dogs and 11, 150 cats. The chart below shows the entry and exit statistics for the county's humane society and animal control shelters.

In this county, animal control has done a average job of returning dogs to owners. Unfortunately, statistics reveal this county to be under-performing in the area of dog and cat adoptions, with animal control doing a very poor job. The county shelter only accounts for 8% of acquired dogs, compared to a national average of 13%. Investigation revealed the animal control shelter is closed on Saturday and Sunday. Management stated, "We're not interested in recycling our problems." The percent of county euthanasias are extremely high compared to the national average. This county euthanizes 6.4% of the total dog population, compared to a national average of 4.6%.

The humane society has dedicated 60% of its resources, personnel and equipment to performing traditional animal control functions because of contempt for county services. Taking these animals in necessitates the destruction of animals to make space in the already full shelter. The general consensus was that abandoning its policy to take in strays would be a departure from its mission to help all stray animals in need by giving them shelter and care. The only problem was it had to kill last week's arrivals to make room for this week's. This was rationalized as society's problem.

Staff personnel had little formal training in medical care, and the agency had no educational program. Employees had no legal authority to perform investigations and seize animals, despite the practice. When spay/neuter surgery was used, they contracted with a veterinarian for a small discount off retail price. Its adoption screening was highly restrictive. Its adoption processing was performed by the kennel staff. Dogs and cats were housed in close proximity, in some cases alongside each other, creating stress. The shelter floors were never sealed to prevent the spread of disease. It made local headlines for refusing to release a dog to purebred rescue.

This organization made attempts to right the ship. It contracted with the American Humane Association to have AHA perform an operational audit. AHA investigated and reported a lack of training and communication, the need for better handling for euthanasia equipment, better record keeping and made other minor suggestions.

Unfortunately, what it didn't tell the agency was, how poorly it was performing as a nonprofit humane organization, how it was duplicating services and how it was misusing vital resources. They didn't define, in no uncertain terms, the organizations failures as animal protectors.

Half the board quit in disgust. A few strong-minded board members took charge and have created considerable ill-will in the community. These individuals have limited experience and knowledge of sound and successful shelter-management practices. Their programs and services are under-performing, yet go uncorrected. It's all explained in the word, "euthanasia." We will give the animals a "loving" death.

There is currently no way well-run shelters can show the money they receive is put to good use. If the organization is well managed, how can it differentiate itself from other organizations and have its work recognized and rewarded with future financial support?

Their programs and services are under-performing, yet go uncorrected. It's all explained in the word, "euthanasia". It's not us, the organization says, it's society. We will give the animals a "loving" death.

Employees are not to blame. They have not been adequately trained or instructed in proper shelter operations. They have no goals, no objectives and a limited understanding of a nonprofit's role. This organization lacks leadership.

The humane society was approached by county officials to contract for animal control services. It is currently planning to incorporate these services into their new shelter building, scheduled to open in 2000. Those poor animals. The only humane care this group can offer is to humanely kill 11,121 out of 13,918 cats and dogs or 80% of animals that enter its facilities.

Consolidation with county animal control will mean the animals will lose a total of 62 cat cages and 122 dog runs in a business where capacity is everything. Euthanasia will continue to be the byword, covering up a multitude of organizational failures.

Future Trends

The average donor demands little, if any, information about the organization's operating effectiveness, financial health, programs, goals and past performance. Donors may respond reactively and compassionately to requests for donations and give *for the animals.* They may give to the largest, the oldest shelters, the ones with the best names or the biggest budgets. Unfortunately, those shelters may not be making the best use of their resources.

Are donors getting the full measure for their investment? Supporters need to know what happens with their donation. Does their money serve the animals? How does the shelter's performance rate compared with national and regional standards? Are governments cost shifting or reducing animal control budgets with the expectation that program costs will be provided by private funders?

More importantly, there is no way that efficient, well-run shelters can show that the money they receive is put to good use. If the organization is well managed, how can they differentiate themselves from other organizations and have their work recognized and rewarded with future financial support?

Nonprofits, including animal shelters, have been created to fill the need when government systems fail. Humane societies and SPCAs are no different. They were founded as a result of limitations in government run animal control shelters. Nonprofit humane societies and SPCAs were a distinct alternative to the space and time limitations which resulted in an inordinate amount of killings at government-run shelters. Unfortunately that distinct nonprofit mission is being slowly blurred as more shelters seek the financial security of animal control contracts.

Donors provide capital and a significant portion of annual revenues to nonprofit shelters. Donors, not the marketplace, nor competition, are the final judge of life, growth, decline or doom for nonprofit animal organizations.

Currently, nonprofit animal shelters are not held accountable to anyone for their performance. Internally, the board of directors' emphasis is on money to fund the shelter's operation. The incentive and reward for executive directors is on fund raising. The more funds they raise, the better. But, are their operations effective? Are the animal needs in their community being met? An objective evaluation system that provides industry "like-kind" comparisons would tell the story.

Recommendations

1. Don't reinforce poorly run programs. Donors to nonprofits must ask the following questions before they donate: 1) How effective is the organization at carrying out its mission? 2) How effective is the organization's program services? 3) What portion of my gift will be used for programs, fund raising and management? 4) Does the organization really need my contribution or does it have enough available assets to do the job?

2. Evaluate and compare shelters as one of three types: private animal shelters, animal control shelters and shelters under 3 years of age (usually have higher fund-raising costs). If such evaluations were to be used, each shelter would be compared to similar shelters of square footage, years of service, budget, animal capacity, euthanasia policy, and other factors. Establishment of national and regional averages will allow shelters to be ranked by program performance.

   This information will identify and support resourceful animal shelters that work ambitiously to save animals. This is what benefactors deem important. Well-informed givers will ask questions and make judgments that will raise operational efficiency and lead to improved levels of performance in animal shelter management. Financial supporters and board directors will unite in purpose. Managers will use evaluations to determine the soundness of past actions and help decide future directions. "Best Practices" will emerge and these programs will be quickly emulated.

3. Obtain nonprofit financial information from the regional IRS office or the state charitable trust unit. You can obtain information on city and county contracts from your local county clerk's office. As Thomas Jefferson said, "Democracy needs vigilance."

   The IRS has changed the accounting rules for nonprofits with the intent of making financial information more uniform so that citizens can compare program costs and gain a better understanding of the organization's financial situation. Eventually, all financial information will be obtainable on every nonprofit through the Internet by the touch of a keystroke.

In the absence of effective nonprofit programs, animal control will be caught in a holding pattern and function to maintain the animal-carrying capacity by killing millions of animals.

Factor Eighteen

Shelters designed for group housing of dogs and cat colonies to decrease kennel stress

Shelter Design

Design decisions for animal shelters are based on formulas which estimate the number of animals impounded annually, adding growth rates and factors which consider the average holding time per animal. Average kennel space is estimated at 24 square feet per run. The computation produces rows of 4-foot cells and chain-link kennel gates that house an isolated wayward dog. Cats and kittens are usually kept in separate rooms in small cat cages.

"Keeping dogs in groups fulfills the dogs need for social interaction and the need to move. Dog fights are seldom and fears of fights and injury are unfounded."
—Mertens and Unshelm

These design decisions, made based on the efficient use of shelter space, maximize the number of animals served. They are expedient for humans to carry out the business of the shelter. Unfortunately, this housing arrangement is not effective for animals. These designs are restrictive and stressful, promoting boredom and lack of motivation in the animal, which can exacerbate behavioral problems.

One of the major reasons animals are euthanized stems from the fact that extended impoundment causes "kennel stress," leading to mental dementia.

Housing for Dogs

A Recent study of German animal shelters, published in *Anthrozoos*, found 51% of German shelters already keep dogs in groups.[26] The 49% that don't, fear fights. The report found that keeping dogs in groups fulfills the dogs' need for social interaction and movement. Dog fights are seldom and fears of fights and injury are unfounded. Dogs housed in groups had closer human/animal relationships creating a significant reduction of noise. Behavioral problems were greater in individually housed dogs by a factor of three to one. Dogs housed in groups took only 9 days to place on average, as opposed to 17 for individually-housed dogs.

After the dogs were adopted, 88% more owners of individually housed dogs complained of problems when compared to owners of dogs housed in groups. Behavior problems, such as separation anxiety, were reduced with group housing.

The study found the presence of fences inhibits normal confrontation and prevents social contact with other dogs. This results in territorial reactions. In traditional dog runs, human contact is reduced to sniffing hands through the kennel bars, as the kennels are constructed in such a way that cleaning and feeding the dogs can be done from a common walkway, without having to enter the cage.

Recommendations

1. Use group dog housing. Bigger kennels are necessary. Kennel attendants must monitor and interact with the dogs.

2. Use open cat rooms with 10 to 13 cats per room size of 15x12 feet. These rooms have ledges, toys, and different places to hide and sleep. Separate kittens and adult cats. Isolate new arrivals for three days before they are introduced to the room. Room attendants must monitor cats for health and behavior, especially with new arrivals. These rooms have been proven to work in various shelters throughout the country. They promote interaction with future adopters and reduce the stress of being in a shelter.

Factor Nineteen
Productive economics

Situation

There is no industry that comes to mind in the for-profit world that works to put itself out of business. Can you imagine a car dealer working to abolish the production of the family sedan?

The Economics of Government Animal Control

Municipal governments are quick to rid themselves of the rising costs of administering animal control programs. Normally, the largest expense of a shelter operation is payroll and benefits, sometimes as high as 70% of expenses. Government programs have the added impact of progressive pay increases and extremely good benefits.

Administrators are squeezed between rising costs on one hand and budget restrictions dictated by politicians who minimize animal programs in favor of human programs. Tax dollars are put into a general fund and prioritized according to need. Animals programs are always underfunded, and as a result, the animals have substandard facilities and less care and service.

Governments are quick to slash funding for animal control, especially during recessions. Normally, this policy — particularly when it comes to spay/neuter — is penny-wise and pound foolish. It has been estimated that one dollar spent on a spay/neuter program will save seven on animal control.[2]

Municipal governments slash animal control funding in the belief that people who care most about animals will pick-up the funding. There has been an increase in cost-shifting, cutting budgets and shifting more responsibility for funding to the private sector. Some government animal control agencies are creating nonprofit corporations to offset costs.

People who care about animal welfare must be diligent in working with community leaders to make sure animal control programs are adequately funded. When community leaders recognize there are large numbers of people who care, they will respond with the funding necessary to deliver sufficient program support.

The Economics of Humane Societies and SPCAs

The main driving force that attracts nonprofit humane societies and SPCAs to animal control contracts is money. Nonprofits must continually make expenses by soliciting private donations. Budgets are, on average, $600,000 a year. These high sums create considerable stress and present weighty demands for successful fund-raising. Normally, 70% of the budget must be raised from private donations; 30% comes from program revenues. Many nonprofit organizations (i.e.,YMCA, Red Cross, Salvation Army) receive annual government grants and institutional funding which comprises a large share of their budgets. That, combined with program revenue, reduces the constant strain for cash from private donors. Nonprofit animal organizations usually enjoy no such luxury.

To achieve progress, humane societies and SPCAs must proceed beyond the level of service the average taxpayer will fund. They must augment animal control programs with proactive programs to reduce birthrates, high volume adoptions and programs that enhance the human/animal bond; programs that care for sick and injured animals; programs the government could not possibly afford, nor administer. These programs are more in keeping with the humane ethic.

95

Fund-raising events do not earn large net revenues until they are well established and attended. The bulk of earnings comes from bequests. Older, established organizations even embark on the risky business of budgeting for bequests. Members of the board of directors are usually chosen for their fund-raising ability and connection to resources in the community.

California Nonprofit Asset Analysis				
Name of Shelter	Assets	Budget	Asset Ratio	Type
San Francisco SPCA	33,345,403	7,209,621	4.6 to 1	Nonprofit Shelter
Holiday Humane Society	12,258,411	338,701	36 to 1	Nonprofit Shelter
Oakland SPCA	11,002,001	2,046,109	5.3 to 1	Nonprofit Shelter
Pasadena Humane Society	9,819,827	2,177,719	4.5 to 1	Animal Control
Santa Barbara Humane Society	9,523,865	1,071,296	8.9 to 1	Nonprofit Shelter
Los Angeles SPCA	7,993,253	3,326,760	2.4 to 1	Animal Control
San Diego Humane Society	7,923,196	2,658,556	3 to 1	Nonprofit Shelter
Peninsula Humane Society	6,628,699	4,604,015	1.4 to 1	Animal Control
Sacramento SPCA	5,651,947	918,011	6 to 1	Nonprofit Shelter
SPCA of Monterey County	5,380,608	1,868,279	2.9 to 1	Animal Control
Living Free Animal Sanctuary	5,317,512	1,320,524	4 to 1	Nonprofit Shelter
Helen Woodward Animal Ctr	4,643,424	2,920,481	1.6 to 1	Nonprofit Shelter
Hum Soc Of Santa Clara Vly	3,265,952	4,936,301	.7 to 1	Animal Control
Marin Humane Society	2,830,120	2,980,429	.9 to 1	Animal Control
Central California SPAC	2,422,528	1,887,016	1.3 to 1	Animal Control
Humane Society of Sonoma Co	1,790,809	1,536,565	1.2 to 1	Animal Control
Pets Unlimited	1,513,678	2,694,200	.6 to 1	Nonprofit Clinic
Santa Cruz SPAC	961,755	1,313,185	.7 to 1	Animal Control
Bakersfield SPCA	914,735	1,106,964	.8 to 1	Animal Control
Hum Society of Pomona Valley	709,108	2,374,210	.3 to 1	Animal Control

As you can see from the table, the public supports nonprofit private shelters. Nearly every nonprofit shelter has at least doubled its annual budget in assets, with the exception of Helen Woodward Animal Center. On the other hand, there are only two nonprofit animal control organizations with an animal control contract that has doubled their yearly budget in assets: Los Angeles SPCA and Pasadena Humane Society have a 2.4 and 4.5 ratio, respectively. Of the eleven nonprofits with animal control contracts, the mean budget-to-asset ratio is 1.5, compared to 4.3 for the nine nonprofit private shelters.

Normally, governments don't include capital improvements when subcontracting animal control. That means when it comes time to improve the shelter or buy new vehicles, it comes out of nonprofit reserve saving accounts. Slowly, reserve assets start to dwindle and nonprofits become trapped in their contracts. A above study of California nonprofits shows a greater concentration of assets in shelters that do not have animal control contracts.

It's a far better strategy to maintain private status and assist animal control by forming an advisory panel and developing programs that complement animal control programs. Or, develop a formal pact similar to that of the city of San Francisco, which formally defines duties and responsibilities between animal control and the SPCA.[45]

The Economics of Veterinarians

Veterinarians are business people. They must make a profit to survive. Spay/Neuter surgery cannot be performed without a licensed veterinarian and it is expensive. Humane groups are trying to remove that financial obstacle. Most veterinarians recognize their moral dilemma and compromise. They enroll in and render some low-cost sterilization for needy pet owners and perform sterilization surgery at full cost for patrons who can afford it, becoming a break-even service. Veterinarian associations usually oppose low-cost spay/neuter clinics and mobile units on the grounds that people who use the low-cost service look like they could afford to pay full retail.

The promotion of vaccine clinics by nonprofit humane societies and SPCAs serve to alienate veterinarians and create opposition instead of cooperation. A far better approach would be to work together and seek cost compromises.

The Economics of Breeders

To most responsible breeders, breeding is not financially attractive. The costs are high for stud fees, health certification (OFA, CERF, VWD), registrations, pedigrees, veterinary exams, X-rays, shots, hearing tests, medications, food, advertising and phone bills. If anything goes wrong with the bitch or her litter, veterinary bills and C-section operations can be expensive. The majority of these people raise animals out of love for the breed. They are trying to produce the finest specimens possible.

On the other hand, backyard and amateur breeders are out for a fast buck. They acquire a popular breed and attempt to recoup their cost and earn some extra money by breeding. They know little about genetics and fail to use pre-mating health x-rays and tests to determine worthiness because of costs. These people are surprised to find the puppies they thought would sell for $400 each are hard to give away.

The Economics of Feral Cats

The issue of feral cats will truly test everyone's definition of humane treatment for animals. The economics of feral cats is complex. To humanely care for a feral cat requires human and financial resources, both in short supply at shelters.

Two methods of dealing with ferals are the TVAR (trap, vaccinate, alter and release) and trap and kill .

The TVAR method requires a trained person to trap, equipment, bait, vaccinations and spay/neuter surgery. Many suggest, as do *Alley Cat Allies,* that colonies be maintained for years. TVAR programs require support by veterinarians who are willing to take on the difficult handling of ferals.

The trap and kill method which is commonly and quietly deployed today by animal control personnel is, on the surface, cost efficient. There are no vaccinations, sterilization surgery and maintenance costs of the colony. However, it doesn't work. Documented studies show that new colonies will re-emerge if there is a food source.

To adequately address the feral cat issue using the TVAR method will require a national effort by tens of thousands of volunteers and additional funding endowed for feral cats. It will undoubtedly require humane organizations to spearhead the program.

The Economics of Dog Trainers

Dog trainers charge from $50 to $175 for their services for six to eight weeks of group class instruction. Hourly amounts are charged by behaviorists who travel to people's houses to modify problem behaviors. To many people, these fees are too high. Instead, they choose to do it themselves. When problems develop, they are quick to blame the dog. The relationship grows bothersome, less time is spent with the dog. The dog is left alone in the backyard, left to stray without identification or eventually relinquished.

Most people who attend dog training classes know the value of education and consider the expense a wise investment. Training programs, however, do not reach the majority of new owners, those who need training the most. Affordable intervention programs are necessary. New owners, especially first-timers, should be required to attend a free two-hour orientation. Every community should have a network of low-cost dog training classes. Instead of citations were the owner pays money, communities should require violators to attend dog training classes.

Conclusion

Pets seldom have animal problems, they have people problems. From birth, companion animals look to humans for their survival. They depend on people for food and safety and put their lives in their owners hands. The relationship is reciprocal. Pets have been serving as companions and best friends to people for centuries. Pets have warmed many cold bodies and many cold hearts. They have given more than they received, as most animal lovers can attest. When the attachment is severed, however, it is unnatural to an animal and a threat to their existence.

The mass destruction of healthy companion animals is caused by many factors. Among the major reasons attributed to owners are failure to spay/neuter, lack of identification, fast-buck breeding, uncommitted and irresponsible owners who fail to resolve minor animal behavior problems or lifestyle changes, stray and abandoned animals "dumped" or left to fend for themselves, accidental mating and low demand for adult, mixed-breed large dogs or mature cats.

The problem lies not only with owners but also with the failure of the system we entrust to manage stray companion animals. Agencies fail to properly define the problem using scientific methodologies. Despite the fact that over 70% of impounded animals are found without identification, ID programs have not been vigorously promoted with the same importance as spay/neuter. Licensing programs are poorly run and animals are adopted from shelters without being spayed or neutered. Feral cats are killed rather than trapped, altered and released. Adoption programs are not aggressively marketed (only 13% of animals are obtained from shelters). Sick and injured animals are not rehabilitated and put up for adoption, but rather destroyed. Educational programs are aimed at grade schools with the hope of salvaging the next generation, when pet-owner behavior needs to be modified, now.[13] Legislation and strict enforcement are strongly promoted, despite evidence suggesting the strategy is misdirected and futile.

Most important, the role of nonprofit organizations (humane societies and SPCAs) is compromised when these organizations assume government contracts and do not devote a large portion of their budget to proactive programs which protects tomorrow's animals from harm.

Nonprofit animal sheltering organizations have the most potential for leading progressive change that will stop the killing of companion animals. When these "humane" agencies (agencies that are founded to protect animals) are involved in killing animals, the inconsistency is not lost on the general public. When constituency wanes, their power to protect the animals is compromised. Being a kill shelter dilutes their full capability for proactive change. They cannot prevent animal killing when the bulk of their budget and their human resources are mired in the day-to-day crisis management of open-admission shelters and the ultimate lack of space which necessitates killing.

To achieve progress, humane societies and SPCAs must proceed beyond the level of service the average taxpayer will fund for government animal control. They must augment animal control programs with proactive programs to reduce birth-rates, increase adoptions, enhance the human/animal bond and care for sick and injured animals. The government could not possibly afford, nor administer these types of programs, which are more in keeping with the humane ethic.

In the absence if these programs, animal control will be caught in a holding pattern and function to maintain the animal-carrying capacity by killing millions of animals.

Over one hundred million people own pets in America. There is tremendous potential for increasing funding, volunteers and adoptions if nonprofits would position themselves as "partners" with government animal control programs, receive transferred animals and develop "adoption-only" operations. Humane societies must not only talk the talk, they must walk the walk. They must deem an animal's life more valuable than its' death. Eventually, as evidenced in San Francisco, government animal control directors will praise the results.

Local community organizations must unite all animal lovers and groups which are deeply concerned by this crisis. United we stand, divided we fail.

Organizations that have shown leadership and achieved remarkable results like North Shore Animal League and San Francisco SPCA must be held up as "best practice" organizations and be readily imitated.

The educational function must not be minimized or compromised. People need to be reached *before* the crisis stage, before the relationship sours, before they unwittingly contribute to the problem. Pet overpopulation is not millions of surplus puppies and kittens born each year. It is one animal or one litter relinquished, it is one animal without identification, it is one animal that is unaltered, it is one animal not loved or cared for. This correlation is rarely understood. Community educational-outreach programs are needed that redeem individuals who unknowingly contribute to the problem by forsaking "just one" animal.[30]

Society's problem is not too many pets, but people's misunderstanding of a cat/dogs nature. Pet owners commonly lack knowledge and awareness of the responsibilities of pet ownership. This leads to pets that are mismanaged and untrained, resulting too often in the abandonment of the animal. Owners need reasonable expectations of feline and canine developmental behavior, as well as means to humanely deal with unwanted behaviors that undermine the human/animal bond. They need a place to turn to when things go wrong.

Combined efforts of animal professionals are needed to instill realistic expectations of companion animal behavior and of the commitments involved in pet ownership. An all-out educational effort must be made by all concerned organizations and individuals, but especially, by veterinarians — the individuals people trust most for advice.

When an animal enters a shelter, specifically an animal control shelter, it's too late. Our national system of animal control has not been developed to re-home these animals sufficiently. Systems have failed to regulate the flow of animals into shelters at a rate where they can adequately care for their needs and redistribute them back into the community. It is the system, by and large, that must be changed with more emphasis on prevention.

Few issues are more important for a pet than having a lifelong home. A nation in which there is a home for every dog and cat born is not impossible to achieve. We are at the dawn of a new age in animal welfare. The challenge for concerned animal people is to make animals more valued in society and their lives more respected.

Tremendous accomplishments and progress have already been recorded by the work of dedicated animal lovers since the dark days of the 1970s when euthanasias reached an all-time high. The killing of companion animals won't end tomorrow, but considerable progress toward that goal could be achieved if we clearly understand the issues and unite in this worthwhile cause.

References

1. AHA. *Animal Sheltering Reporting Study*: 1985-1992 Entry/Exit numbers, American Humane Association

2. Animal People National study of veterinary hospitals July/Aug. 1994

3. Animal People Shelter Data December 1997

4. Animals' Agenda The Role of Animal Shelters 1997 Mar/Apr. 40-46

5. Arkow PA. The humane society and the human-animal bond: Reflections on the broken bond., *Symposium on the Human-Companion Animal Bond 455-466*

6. Arkow PA new look at pet overpopulation. *Anthrozoos* 1995; 8:178-179

7. Arkow, P. Animal control laws and enforcement *J Am Vet Med Assoc 1991; 198,7:1164-1172*

8. Arluke A. Coping with euthanasia: A case study of shelter culture *J Am Vet Med Assoc 1991*; 198:7:1176-1180

9. Avanzino R . Pet overpopulation and human education in schools and communities *J Am Vet Med Assoc* 1991:198;7:1237-1241

10. AVMA. U.S. pet ownership and pet overpopulation. Center for information management, Schaumburg, IL

11. Brestrup C The killing cure *The Animals Agenda* Sept/Oct 1997 44-45

11. California Council of Companion Animal Advocated Results from pet overpopulation III

12. California Deparment of Health Animal Control Statistics 1970 to 1996

13. Caras R. One generation away from humanity. *J Am Vet Med Assoc* 1993;202:910-912

14. Carter CN Pet population control: Another decade without solutions? *J Am Vet Med Assoc 1990;197:192-195*

15. Cloud DF Working with breeders on solutions to pet overpopulation *J Am Vet Med Assoc* 1993 202:6:912-914

16. Faulkner, LC Dimensions of the pet population problem *J Am Vet Med Assoc 1975;166:477-478*

17. Garvin D. Public perception: the AKC and purebred dogs. *AKC Gazette* 111: 58-60

18. Humane Society of the United States National Statistics on Pet Ownership Shelter Sense May 1993

19. Jochle W Pet population control in Europe *J Am Vet Med Assoc* 1991 198:7:1225-1230

20. Johnson K Survey report and analysis of San Diego and Santa Clara pet population *National Pet Alliance* 1995 web site

21. Kidd AH, Kidd RM, George CC. Successful and unsuccessful pet adoptions. *Psychol Rep* 1992;70:547-561

22. Luke C. Animal shelter issues *J Am Vet Med Assoc* 1996 208:4:524-527

23. MacKay CA. Veterinary practitioners' role in pet overpopulation. *J Am Vet Med Assoc 1993;202,6,918-921*

24. Massachusetts SPCA Survey on Pet Ownership Shelter Sense May 1993

25. Manning,AM and Rowan, AN. Companion animal demographics and sterilization status: Results from a survey of four Massachusetts towns. 1192; *Anthrozoos* 5: 192-201

26. Mertens PA Unshelm J Effects of group and individual housing on the behavior of kennelled dogs in animal shelters *Anthrozoos* 1996 Vol IX No 1: 40-50

27. Miller DD, Staats SR, Partlo C, Rada K. Factors associated with the decision to surrender a pet to an animal shelter *J Am Vet Med Assoc* 1996 209:4:738-742

28. Miller-Dowling J. Stitely C Killing ourselves over the euthanasia debate 1997 *Animal Sheltering* Sept/Oct 4-15

29. Miller J. The Domestic Cat J Am Vet Med Assoc 1998

30. Moulton C, Wright P, Rindy K The role of animal shelters in controlling pet overpopulation. *J Am Vet Med Assoc* 1991; 198:1172

31. Nassar R. Understanding the dynamics of your community's pet population. *Veterinary Medicine* 1986; 81: 1120-1126

32. Nassar R. Fluke J Pet population dynamics an community planning for animal welfare and animal control *J Am Vet Med Assoc* 1991 198:7:1160-1163

33. Nassar R Mosier J Projections of pet population from census demographic data *J Am Vet Med Assoc* 1991; 198, 7, 1157-1159

34. Olson PN, Moulton C, Nett TM et al Pet overpopulation: a challenge for companion animal veterinarians in the 1990s *J Am Vet Med Assoc 1991; 198:1151-1152*

35. Olson PN, Johnson SD. New developments in small animal population control *J Am Vet Med Assoc* 1993; 202;6:904-908

36. Patronek GJ. Development of a model for estimating the size and dynamics of the pet dog population. *Anthrozoos* 1994; 7:25-41

37. Patronek GJ, Glickman LT and Moyer MR. Population Dynamics and risk of euthanasia for dogs in an animal shelter. 1995; *Anthrozoos* 8:31-43

38. Patronek GJ and Rowan AR. Editorial - Determining dog and cat numbers and population dynamics *Anthrozoos* 1995; 8,4:199-205

39. Patronek GJ, Glickman LT, Beck AM. McCabe GP and Ecker C. Risk factors of relinquishment of cats to an animal shelter. *J Am Vet Med Assoc* 1996; 2\09:582-588

40. Robinson WR How to keep a humane society hospital out of your community *Veterinary Economics* 1990:32-41

41. Rollin BE. Social ethics, veterinary medicine, and the pet overpopulation. *J Am Vet Med Assoc* 1991;198:1153-1156

42. Rowan AN Shelters and pet overpopulation: A statistical black hole *Anthrozoos* Vol 5 No3 140-143

43. Rowan AN, Williams J. The success of companion animal management programs: A review. *Anthrozoos* 199x;Vol 1, No 2: 110

44. Salman MD, New JG, Scarlett JM, Kass PH, Ruch-Gallie R, Hetts S. Human and Animal Factors Related to Relinquishment of Dogs and Cats in 12 Selected Animal Shelters in the U.S. Journal of Applied Animal Welfare Science 3 207-226

45. San Francisco SPCA Building a no-kill city 1998

46. Schneider RB. Vaida ML Survey of canine and feline population: Alameda and Contra Costa counties, California *J Am Vet Med Assoc* 1975; 166:481-486

47. Schneider RB. Observations on the overpopulation of dogs and cats. *J Am Vet Med Assoc* 1975; 167:281-284

48. Stockner PK The economics of spaying and neutering: Market forces and owners values affecting pet population control *J Am Vet Med Assoc* 1991 198:7:1180-1182

49. Strand PL The pet owner and breeder's perspective on overpopulation *J Am Vet Med Assoc* 1993 202;6:921-927

50. Theran P. Early-age neutering of dogs and cats *J Am Vet Med Assoc* 1993 202:6:914-917

51. Weirauch R The road to success: Have you checked the map lately? *Animal Sheltering* 1996 Jan/Feb 6-14

52. Patronek GJ, Glickman LT, Beck AM. McCabe GP and Ecker C. Risk factors for relinquishment of dogs to an animal shelter. *J Am Vet Med Assoc* 1996;

Appendix
Computing Your Regional Statistics

Many areas look at their own shelter statistics to determine effectiveness. It is important to look at the *entire region* to get a true picture of the community surplus animal problem. Additionally, many shelters are computing the number of adoptable animals that were adopted (in response to no-kill initiatives). This practice is subjective and very misleading to the public. It's open to exaggeration that is used to advance political agendas and wrongfully gives the impression that only sick and aggressive animals are being euthanized. A study found a major agency quoting that 98% of adoptable animals were adopted. Closer examination revealed the region to be euthanizing 5% of the total number of animals in their area (the national average). This is a self-serving way of depicting data and it grossly misrepresents the situation and defuses the sense of public urgency.

To properly compute your regional dog & cat statistics use the following:

	Number	National Average
Human Population in Region		
Occupied Housing in Region (US Census Bureau or local library)		
DOGS		
Dog Population (est. using Am Vet Med. Assoc. formula for your state)		
Dog Licenses Sold		
% of Dogs w/ License (Divide No. of dogs into No. licenses sold)		33%
Number of Dogs Obtained Each Year (Multiply total dogs x .12)		
Dog Impoundment's / % AC pick-ups/Owner Reling/public surrenders		
% Rate of Dog Population (divide total dogs into total impoundment's)		9%
Number of Dogs Adopted at Shelters		
Shelter Market Share (Divide total dogs obtained into total adoptions)		14%
Shelter Dog Adoption Rate (Divide dog impoundment's into adoptions)		25%
Dogs Returned to Owner		
Dog Return to Owner Rate (Divide impoundment's into dog returns)		14%
Euthanized		
Dog Euthanasia Rate (Divide Impoundment's into euthanized)		61%
% of All Dogs in Region Euthanized (Divide total dogs into euthanized)		5%
CATS		
Cat Population (Owned) (est. using AVMA formula for your state)		
Feral, Unowned Cat Population (+40% to 60%)		
Total Cat Population (Add above)		
Number of Cats Obtained Each Year (Cat population x .12)		
Cat Impoundment's AC Pic-ups/Owner Reling/Humane Surrenders		
% Rate of Cat Population (divide owned cats into total impoundment's)		7%
Total Number of Cats Adopted at Shelters		
Adoption Rate (Divide cat impoundment's into adoptions)		19%
Shelter Market Share (Divide total cats obtained into total adoptions)		12%
Cats Returned to Owner		
Cat Return to Owner Rate (Divide impoundment's into cat RTO's)		1%
Euthanized		
Cat Euthanasia Rate (Divide Total Impoundment's into euthanized)		80%
% of Owned Cats Euthanized (Divide owned cats into euthanized)		6%
Total Regional Combined Dogs & Cats		Loc / Nat Avg
Impounded		
Dogs		
Cats		
Adopted		29% / 20%
Returned To Owner		10% / 11%
Euthanized		61% / 69%
Animal Control Cost per capita		$5 per Capita

ORDER FORM

_____ **Choosing & Caring for a Shelter Dog** $12 ea = _____
_____ **Save Our Strays** $15 ea = _____
_____ **Board of Directors Handbook** $15 ea = _____
_____ **"Pet Overpopulation Town Hall Meeting" video** $25 ea = _____
_____ **"Save Our Strays" Audio Tape** $10 ea = _____

Look for **Save Our Strays** Caps, Decals, Stickers
T-shirts, Coffee Mugs, Posters,
Buttons and Magnets for sale on website
Coming Soon! _The Adventures of Ranger, Humane Education for Children_

*Shipping = _____

Please enclosed a check made out to **CLC Publishing**   **Total** $ _____

Other services available by Bob Christiansen: Town Hall Meeting on Pet Overpopulation, Board of Directors Retreats, Organizational Performance Evaluation. Call for more information.

Ship to Name: _____
Address: _____
City/State/Zip: _____
Telephone: _____ Contact: _____

SPECIAL QUANTITY DISCOUNTS:

50% Off Books are available at special discounts for bulk purchases (12 and up) for animal-related charitable activities and organizations Call **CLC PUBLISHING** for additional discounts on major quantity purchases (60+).

California residents please add 7.75% Sales Tax
*Shipping charge: Please add $3 for first book and $.50 for each additional book up to 14. $10 = 15 to 60.

Visit our website: saveourstrays.com
Email: rgc@saveourstrays.com
CLC PUBLISHING • P.O. Box 10515 • Napa, California 94581
(707) 226-5574